Baghdad Sketches

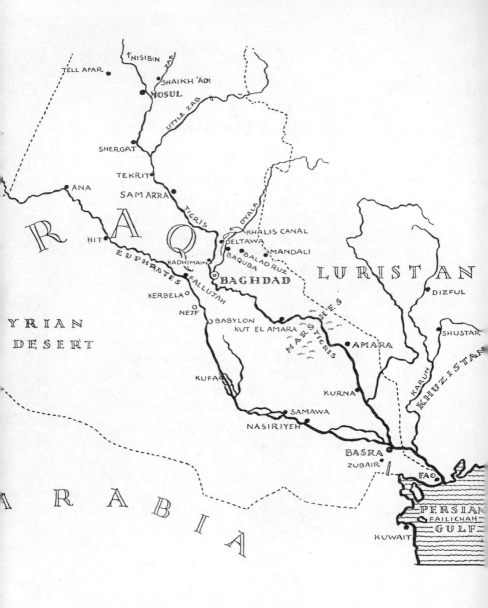

FREYA STARK

BAGHDAD SKETCHES

INTRODUCTION BY
BARBARA KREIGER

TᴍP

THE MARLBORO PRESS / NORTHWESTERN
EVANSTON, ILLINOIS

The Marlboro Press/Northwestern
Northwestern University Press
Evanston, Illinois 60208-4170

Baghdad Sketches copyright © 1938 by E. P. Dutton & Co., Inc.
Introduction copyright © 1992 by Barbara Krieger. This edition
published in 1992 by the Marlboro Press. The Marlboro
Press/Northwestern edition published 1996. All rights reserved.

10 9 8 7 6

Printed in the United States of America

ISBN 0-8101-6023-4

Library of Congress Cataloging-in-Publication Data

Stark, Freya.
    Baghdad sketches / Freya Stark ; introduction by Barbara
Krieger.
        p. cm.
    Originally published: Marlboro, Vt. : Marlboro Press, 1992.
    ISBN 0-8101-6023-4 (pbk. : alk. paper)
    1. Baghdad (Iraq)—Description and travel. 2. Iraq—
Description and travel. 3. Iraq—Social life and customs. 4.
Stark, Freya—Journeys—Iraq. I. Title.
DS79.9.B25S73 1996
956.7'47—dc20   96-31050
                                                                  CIP

From
a Dusty City
to
the Green Hills of Asolo
this Book
is Dedicated.

Contents

The Making of a Traveller

In the fall of 1928, a thirty-five-year-old Englishwoman set out on her first journey to the Middle East. Bolstered by a command of Arabic, a fair knowledge of Pharsi, and the ir-repressible drive that would mark over half a century as trav-eller and explorer, Freya Stark spent the better part of the next four years in Iraq and Persia, investigating ancient and medieval sites and writing for the *Baghdad Times* a series of pieces that would eventually emerge as *Baghdad Sketches*, her first in a long line of distinguished travel books.

In the course of the next three decades, Stark would make a name for herself as traveller, writer, and Arabist, and dur-ing World War II the British government would make use of her expertise and assign her to a post in Aden. The coinci-dence of her travel years and the emergence of the Middle East as a crucial element in the world order made Stark a valuable resource to her government and in an informal way turned her into something of a career diplomat. She sus-pected as early as 1921 that "the most interesting things in the world were likely to happen in the neighborhood of *oil*." But her love of the East pre-dated thoughts of a career and persisted with no regard on her part for its utility. Imagi-natively, Stark had lived in the East since age nine, when an aunt innocently gave her a copy of *The Arabian Nights*. Her taking up Arabic when she was twenty-eight, in 1921, seems as much a completion of the childhood experience as the beginning of the adult one. A few years later she read Charles Doughty's *Arabia Deserta*, after which her eyes were turned unalterably to the ancient lands east of the Mediterranean.

There were less definable influences, too, and it could be that her gift of travel grew out of a nature adventurous by instinct; she was not yet four when she first set out, only to be discovered on the road to Plymouth by a postman, who persuaded her that she might need a little money for her journey. And then there was the early pattern of her family life; her parents separated when she and her sister were still young, and the two girls frequently travelled between their father's beloved Dartmoor countryside and their mother's home in northern Italy.

Beyond that was a keen intellectual curiosity and restlessness, and one feels the young woman looking for a direction for her very considerable energy and talent. She showed promise as a painter, but her artist parents steered her away from painting. In music, her mother, an accomplished pianist, discouraged her by insisting on either rigorous dedication or nothing. Stark's beloved sister Vera, who would die when only thirty-two of an infection brought on by a miscarriage, later resented that they had never been encouraged to pursue any particular activity. But Freya felt differently, and later explained: "I am grateful now for this emptiness of our youth, and especially for the habit of solitude, which is so hard later to acquire, and is to the spirit what a private room is to the mind, giving it space to grow."

Stark was a passionate reader, and when she was nineteen and enrolled at Bedford College in London, she came under the influence of the medievalist W.P. Ker. He encouraged her to write, and though her poetry did not show the distinct promise she hoped it would, it was clear that in writing she had found a home. But she hadn't yet discovered her subject, and the frequent interruptions by which her young adulthood were marked—the First World War, a four-year battle with a severe ulcer, poverty—delayed her long dreamt of departure almost more than she could bear. When it seemed nothing else could detain her, her father, by then living in British Columbia, suffered a stroke; only his insistence that she go east for herself and not west for him released her.

So it was that she departed in 1928, and as she set out, one feels her uncaged, as though her spirit and imagination were suddenly set free. Still weak from an operation and from having spent half of the last four years in bed, filled with an abiding sorrow over the loss of her sister, tugged at by guilt for not going to her father, she flew to the East as a bird pursues its annual migration, instinct filling in for all she did not know.

In Baghdad European women were not a rarity, but one such as Stark had hardly been seen there before. With the notable exception of the famous orientalist Gertrude Bell, who had died two years before Stark's arrival, the other Englishwomen there were the wives of British civil servants, devoted to convention as Stark was to independence from it. She found herself on the fringe of their community, and despite her determination to make a life for herself, a year after reaching Iraq she wondered with some melancholy when she would find her place. She felt her life was passing quickly and sensed that people found little value in what she was writing, a series of pieces for the *Baghdad Times* that would soon become these *Baghdad Sketches*. No one seemed to respond to her as an individual. Kindly people, she noted, felt sorry for her; the others simply disapproved of a woman on her own. With the honesty that always characterized her writing, she recorded: "To be just middle-aged with no particular charm or beauty and no position is a dreary business." With poignant self-doubt she wrote to her mother: "If only I could eventually find some work that would make me feel settled and interested; I hope it may be: but no one seems to want women very much."

The Making of a Traveller

The predicament her sex presented was to repeat itself with endless variations in her encounters with the Moslem world, and in general she accepted the male attitude toward her with good humor. But at one point she confessed from Persia: "None of the men you meet here on the road say good day to so inferior an object as a woman . . . [The] truth is I am lonely and feel worn out with the strain of being considered a phenomenon all the time." But a phenomenon she continued to be, and while perhaps the strain never wore off, she did learn to take advantage of her position. Indeed her double exclusion, as a European and as a woman, defined for her a singular place on the margin. Unlike male European travellers, she had access to the little-observed Arab harem and has written movingly of life behind the veil. On the practical side, she remarked that being a woman may have saved her life on more than one occasion, when a man in her place might have been murdered.

Stark insisted that her early life had trained her to be indifferent to circumstances and had taught her the importance of self-reliance. Though she claims to have wanted approval, she was never willing to sacrifice anything important to get it. Her interest was unremittingly in the individual, and she balked at labels or categories. She knew that her travelling alone upset people, but she quipped, "One can't wait to be quite decrepit to enjoy life." Rebel and eccentric in this way, though never by design or for the effect, she went her own way and learned to live with the disapprobation of her compatriots.

In Italy once again, Stark spent the next two years preparing for a difficult trip to the southern coast of Arabia, where she hoped to follow an ancient incense route. There she fell seriously ill with measles, dysentery, and heart complications, and by any account was lucky to have survived. Yet she never became more timid, and continued to expose herself to danger rather than trim her expectations of a journey. For Stark, risk-taking was the essence of a life worth living. Whether high in her beloved mountains or far removed in the vast desert, she abandoned caution in pursuit of her goal. But she was no thrill-seeker and never sought out danger for itself. She took chances as a way of expressing, or perhaps discovering, her freedom, and freedom from the fear of death was her high aspiration. She wrote early in her career of wishing to attain "the sense of death as a new and wonderful adventure." For success would mean "the absolute liberation from fear, which is a form of slavery."

Stark's whole career may be defined as a quest for freedom. Freedom was risk-taking because in her eyes the ideal of the individual had to do with a refusal to compromise about "what one holds to be the best truly. Sometimes it is difficult to know—and one gives up what seems a great deal for what is only a dim possibility, never probably to be realized." Stark lived for those dim possibilities. They were her horizons, the distant, intangible places that her heart sought out—perhaps unattainable, even unknowable, yet somehow there and providing direction. On this matter, the distinction between Stark the person and Stark the traveller is erased.

About the relation of a journey to a destination she had a lot to say. To the true traveller, it is never merely the destination that is sought. The horizon, she insisted, is irresistible. She speaks with distaste for modern travel, the point of which "is to give people a glimpse of the exotic places without the least bit of inconvenience to themselves." The true traveller "still values the journey for its own sake." In fact, the journey itself is "the main ingredient of serious travel." She did indeed seek out places, but though they were important in themselves, they were also part of a strategy to spur her on when the going got rough. But the notion of arrival is foreign to a traveller like Stark. There is no more arrival on a journey than there is in life. The journey is a reflection of the person in the making.

The Making of a Traveller

Reflecting on what she perceived to be the two essential types of people, the so-called wild and tame, Stark noted: "Every wild animal lives in a state of danger, which means deciding all the time, while the very essence of tameness is the absence of any need for decision. The wild soul is perhaps conscious—as I certainly am always conscious—of the intrinsic danger of life, which is hidden from the domesticated." There is no self-aggrandizement in her distinction; she is simply attempting to account for her own response to life, which generally seemed at odds with her peers'. She further applied the distinction to travel, which for her was as intense a mental activity as a physical one. The domesticated, he says with the biting wit that characterizes her writing, suffers from a park precinct mentality. "What it likes is to have the views of the outside brought in to vary the sheltered panorama; and, though it may travel from the Crystal Palace to Timbuctoo, the park precinct will never be abandoned. The genuinely wild is not intertested in 'seeing the world'; it is exclusively interested in *being*, it digests the world as a cow chews its cud not for what the grass looks like but for what it does inside. This hunger is insatiable, until the desire itself for being shall pass away; and these creatures travel, even if they are sitting motionless and chained." The true traveller, she claims, is interested in the internal world, in the inner effect of the external. Put to the test, Stark wrote to her publisher from her sick-bed in southern Arabia in 1938: "I am a poor thing and I have been lying in bed and thinking that I must give up exploring and Settle Down for ever and ever: I don't think I really mind—it really is *how* and not *what* one sees that matters."

The secret of travel lies not merely in the giving over of oneself to the journey; travel demands a mental readiness to leave one's past behind, and to keep the mind blank for the new to be received. There is a difference, Stark maintained, even in a mere stroll, "if the outer world seeps in with silences and leisures, and words are not thrown like stones into a pool, to break all reflection with private affairs." Travel for Stark, as it was for all the most interesting travellers, was an interior affair, an encounter with herself as well as with other people. Her travels gave her the opportunity to experience the solitude that was so crucial to her well-being. Solitude, she would observe in *The Valleys of the Assassins*, "is the one deep necessity of the human spirit to which adequate recognition is never given in our codes. It is looked upon as a discipline or penance, but hardly ever as the indispensable, pleasant ingredient it is to ordinary life."

The freedom she sought was paired with what she called loneliness—not to be associated with sorrow, but rather with this very solitude by which we "weigh our values at leisure . . . [and] judge them anew in the presence of things almost eternal." Her journeys never failed to test her in this way, so that she was a different person for the miles she went. Certainly she had a great love of travel for its own sake, a need to be out there where her spirit could exercise. And no doubt too the distant world was often more congenial than the home hearth to her way of experiencing. But perhaps most important, Stark found in travel an external way of being that corresponded to her singular relationship with life.

Stark was not a carrier of banners, no matter what they read, but it would be no surprise if one day she were adopted by like-minded women as an early example of what a woman with faith in herself could accomplish. She would marry briefly later on, but at thirty-nine she wrote to a friend: "I used to feel that I had missed the real reason of life by not marrying, and was out of the stream in a backwater as it were. But I now feel this is not so . . . we are just stepping into a wider world and need not feel lonely, except in the ways that pioneers are lonely. Life is easier for married people, but I think it ought to be if anything richer for us, so long as we take it with full hands and not with the inferiority sense that has so often ruined the life of spinsters." No one who reads Freya Stark can doubt that she held out two hands to life. What she grasped only she finally knows, but she did so devotedly and with love.

—Barbara Kreiger

Foreword

Eight of these sketches are the product of a recent visit to Iraq: but as for the rest—written to amuse the readers of the Baghdad Times—*so many of them my friends—they were not intended for a book: like straws thrown casually into some propitious earthly strata, they have become fossilized by accident, not by any innate permanence of their own.*

They were meant to give a picture of daily life in Baghdad in 1931. *Even then, under its Western make-up, the features of the Caliphs' City were growing dim: six years have passed, and the outlines are fainter still, the uniformity of progress more inexorable, the benefits of civilization more difficult to control: what was written as gossip can soon be read as History, like many a trifle before it, for the world of* 1931 *is already of the past.*

Whether these Western floods, to which all her sluices are open, come to the East for baptism or drowning, is hard to say. Total immersion in any case she is bound to submit to and we—who love the creature—wait with some misgiving to see in what condition her regenerated head will appear above the waters; we stand upon the shore and collect such oddments as we find floating in chaos—her customs, religions, her clothes and trinkets and some, alas! of her virtues. We snatch them as they drift for ever out of sight, and encase them in an armour of words—and by so doing, not unhopeful of the future, yet wage our little losing battle against the fragilities of Time.

1937.   FREYA STARK

Baghdad Sketches

The Desert Route

In a very short time a railway will link Baghdad with Europe.

Even now the crossing of the desert is an everyday affair, and although the Nairn Motor Transport do what they can, and cook your breakfast-sausage romantically for you in the open desert over a fire of camelthorn, with an old paraffin box ready to help in case of need, they do not quite succeed, one must admit, in giving the true nomadic feeling to any except most innocent travellers.

In the place where the old Arabian singers saw the three blackened hearthstones of the Beloved in the deserted camp, we now pass derelict skeletons of cars, and a notice will soon be required—indeed is required already—to beg people not to strew paper bags about the desert. But even so the great space holds its own, and some dim feeling of immensity comes through the thick glass of the long six-wheeler to its sleepy inhabitants. And if one desires a little less of comfort and a little more of the unexpected, one can always bargain with one of those little reckless native cars that rush about in the wake of the larger convoy.

In the open desert, indeed, there is romance even in the motor.

There is no high road except such as is made by the track of previous wheels and is blotted out by every rain.[1] Far and near, before you and behind, cars of every kind speed over the uninhabited earth. They roll its sands in spirals like a pillar of cloud behind them, or shine with headlights, like a column of

---

[1] No longer so now.

fire by night. At the last French post you can examine at leisure the desert traffic: lorries top-heavy under their loads, which sail the sands like broad-bowed merchant vessels and lurch from side to side; pilgrim vans for Mekka, fully packed with humanity on hard seats in a sort of grilled cage, and many packages on the ceiling; the long grey chassis of the Nairn, travelling in respectable seclusion; and in and out of all these greater monsters, the indiscriminate crowd of small cars, Chevrolet, Morris, Fiat, Ford, in every stage of smartness and dilapidation, but chiefly the latter, and with every variety of box and bundle bulging at back and sides.

The desert lies in front; not sand, but hard red earth, with beds of flints strewn over its low heights. The camels of the Rualla, in dun-coloured herds, drift here in hundreds over its green fringe. That comes to an end, and presently there is nothing, not even thin spikes of gray grasses in the hollows. White sheets of mirage, like a shallow lake country far away, melt in the horizon, run into each other, recede as we approach. The land curves gently, in waves so smooth, it is as if each easy rise were but the rounded bosom of the earth, each gentle dip but her soft movement as she slips through space; and the hours go with nothing to count them by but the fierce steps of the sun, the Lord Absolute in his own land. He goeth forth as a strong man to run a race, and there is nothing hid from the heat thereof. He beats almost intolerably on my lap, which the shadow of the car's hood will not cover.

I am going the cheap way, being poor and also democratic by nature. An Armenian with a big hat and nose and very small eyes collared me as I got out of the boat at Beyrout and inveigled me into this little car. He promised me the company of two English ladies and a colonel. The two ladies have turned out to be Greeks from Constantinople settled in Aleppo and now going to visit a brother who is a pastry-cook in Baghdad, where I have promised to call on them. The only other traveller is a young Levantine in a béret, very obliging and polite, but not at all like a colonel in any army. We are all very contented, and share each other's provisions, and the ladies give me water from a canvas bag kept cool by the moving air. This is my first journey across the desert; I have no useful knowledge.

Nine hours we have been speeding along; the going is remarkably smooth; the little car excellent, and the chauffeur also; we spend our twilight racing the Nairn down an open wadi; from all sides the far-scattered convoy gathers together towards Rutba Wells. And now in the darkness which meets us so swiftly from the east, the light of Rutba shines above its high-windowed walls and four round towers. The gate is always kept fast. But a sentry is there to say the word; an Arab tribal policeman with a red cloak over his khaki, the star of Iraq a little tipsily over one eye; his red kafieh and black 'igal, his military boots and neat puttees, long Arab face, black plaits and meeting eyebrows, make a typical enough mixture of East and West.

Rutba is the palace planted in the wilderness when Aladdin's uncle rubbed the lamp; how else can it have got there? It is 200 empty miles from anywhere. It has beds to sleep in and waiters who spontaneously think of hot water. You walk into a room and dine on salmon mayonnaise and other refinements and read notices on walls like those of an English club house in the country. The British, returning from summer leave, are all talking shop or shootings and look nice and clean. I have not felt so near home since the day when, coming down upon Jordan from Hauran, we discovered marmalade in Jericho.

Meanwhile the Aleppo ladies and such eat whatever happens to be inside their strange bundles and wait in heaps in the cars in the yard. As I walked across to my room I peered at their dim untidy dishevelment where they lay asleep. I think it is not really good manners to be more comfortable than my fellow-travellers; it is a sentiment which never gets put into practice, but I had felt apologetic about it when I went to dine. They would have been far from happy in that aloof British atmosphere: they like a sympathetic world where people talk to anyone at all times without being introduced: but one might feel excluded all the same, sitting there in the starlight while others sit at dinner; nationalisms, bolshevisms, all sorts of difficult plants, grow during such cold meditations: and how is one to prevent it? So I thought, getting into a very comfortable bed, where, however, I was not allowed to rest in peace for long, for various members of the party called me at intervals with unfounded warnings of departure. When I crept out for the third time, I was feeling like a bolshevik myself.

It was 1 a.m. The yard was wrapped in peaceful slumber. The convoy had no thought of leaving till four. The sentry at the gate in his cloak explained that he could not open for less than two cars, three being the regulation minimum; it seemed a reasonable attitude. A few dim sleepy figures lifted their heads from the ground to corroborate and join in the discussion: could we find no other car to go? Two months before a man went alone and got lost; long afterwards he was found dead in the desert, his petrol tin empty: so said the sentry, accentuating the horrors of his tale with wild black eyebrows; the barrel of his rifle shone in the lantern light among the sleeping cars; the listeners on the ground nodded their heads and murmured in chorus. But our chauffeur had made up his mind. He appeared presently with a friend from Damascus, master of a semi-derelict Ford, and with the word of the Shaikh of the convoy, who gave permission to go if we promised to bring our feeble consort safely through. The gate was opened. "God be with you," said the policeman. In no time the light of Rutba was swallowed up behind us: and nothing human left in sight except a faint gleam from our consort ahead. This also soon lost itself.

The desert felt immense at night. The lop-sided moon was setting between two hills with a faint and dusky glow, fit light for two dead worlds to look upon each other. But in the East we had the rising stars against us: one after another they sprang from the dark horizon and climbed into the cold air: Orion, green and brilliant, swung across the arch of heaven on our right hand.

Meanwhile our consort was giving trouble. We finally found her panting on a wrong track, and had to hoot at intervals to keep her straight before us. Then she broke down. After some consultation, we prodded her with our radiator from behind: it was a strange way of dealing with desert transport, but this gentle encouragement appeared to be all that she required, and we went on gaily side by side. When the dawn broke, we saw the lands of the Euphrates and dark patches of palms.

Passports and customs at Ramadi, Fallujah's bridge of boats, a run over the flat land between the rivers, and then Baghdad with all but its sand-coloured minarets hidden in palm groves. It seems incredible, but we are there.

An Introduction from Damascus

Baghdad, if you ask your friends about it, has one remarkable peculiarity. It is impossible to live there for less than a pound a day. I was told so by all the well informed. And as a pound a day is altogether unthinkable as far as my travels are concerned, I looked despondently at the map and thought the matter over.

There it was, a little conglomeration of red squares with the blue line of the Tigris running through it: and the index classed it among the Towns of First Importance. Surely, I thought, even in a town of First Importance, *everybody* cannot have a pound a day for housekeeping. I made up my mind to disregard the people who know and to ask my Bahai friend in Damascus as I went through.

This Bahai is one of the kindest men in the world. He is known as Ashraf the Indian, and lived for many years in Baghdad before he settled in Damascus as a tanner. I made his acquaintance rather unexpectedly, for I found him one day when I returned to my room from a walk, sitting by my dressing-table together with a very pretty English girl whom I had met the night before at dinner. She had been staying in Haifa with an Oxford friend of hers, a granddaughter of Baha' Ullah, and had now come with introductions to Damascus. Ashraf the Indian in his hospitable way invited her to stay in his home "by the Khan of the Water Melons in the Street of the Mill," and had entertained her with much honour but in complete silence, for neither spoke the other's language.

She sat through the morning and half the afternoon in a circle of respectful and taciturn Elders, drinking cups of coffee at intervals, and being served with the very best the little household could afford; then, unable to bear it any longer, she fled to me for help, bringing her host along with her. He, in his gentle flowery way, explained the situation, which had evidently been just as exhausting to the Arab performers.

I returned the call next morning to rescue the distressed one, and found myself welcomed with effusion in one of those secluded courts which you enter through a low passage from a back street of the Moslem quarter. In this fanatical part of the town, in 1927 when the French had made the sight of Europeans unpopular in Damascus, Ashraf afterwards told me he had found no little difficulty in keeping a foreign guest at all: but apart from his natural generosity and kindness, a religious sect is a sure haven in the East to all who may belong or—as far as my experience of Bahais goes—whose friends may belong; it seemed to me as I stepped into the best room hung with cotton shades, and greeted the silent assembly— Kurds, Indians, Moslem converts—that such gatherings in quiet courts behind closed gates can have changed very little since the days when Paul stayed in this very city in the house of Ananias. From one house to another, in countries far apart, through all the strange complicated network of the East, you are sent from friends to friends, helped and advised, and hidden if need be from the eyes of your enemies. And so when I returned to Damascus after a year, my first thought was to go to the house near the Khan of the Water Melons in the Street of the Mill and tell them of my plans.

I had become a friend long before this, and the three small girls who were playing in the courtyard opened the gate and danced round me like little dusky fairies, and slipping their tiny dark hands tinkling with bangles into mine, led me to their mother. She also is small and graceful and dusky-skinned. She greeted me with both hands outstretched. Ashraf was away; she would send for him.

He had been ill, she said. A bullet had gone through his

cheek, on the bit of road west of Hauran as you motor up from Galilee, when he was returning from a pilgrimage to Haifa. After shooting him, they had robbed him, but that did not matter so much; and thanks be to God, he was well now.

She took me into the guest room, stuffy with velvet chairs and printed Indian covers and atrocious photographs, and introduced me to a dim lady sitting there with two children—an unattractive woman with neck and head swathed in white and a black veil over, like the picture of Saint Theresa, whom, however, she resembled in no other respect. Her business at the moment was to look for a wife for the Vizier of an Indian Sultan, who was travelling for pleasure in Syria. But she was much too preoccupied with her own affairs and the thought of what she could possibly get out of me, to give any details of this interesting transaction. She was like a blight in the friendly atmosphere of the little Indian family, where one is liked for oneself and where this tiresome business of East and West can be forgotten for a while. With her it could not be forgotten. And a dreadful thing happened.

Her little girl had watched the three children of the house sitting at ease round my chair and on my knees, fingering my scarf and the various objects which belonged to me. Presently, very shyly and inch by inch, she left her small brother and crept up to join us. I had just reached out an arm to gather her into the group, when the woman leaped up, sprang across the room, seized her, flung her to the ground, and stamped on her. It was a horrid sight. It took a few seconds to beat her off, for she was like one possessed, and by that time the child was so terrified that it could neither hear nor understand. It shrank from its mother with a fear that was sickening to see.

"What is the matter?" said I when I could speak, for I was choking with anger.

"She made a face at her brother," the woman explained, noticing at last and gazing with obvious surprise at my rage.

An Introduction from Damascus

Our gentle hostess, much disturbed, hastened to send the little sobbing one out into the yard to play.

"We do not treat a dog like that, much less a child," said I, still quivering with fury.

The woman looked at me open-mouthed.

"She must learn to respect her brother," she said.

And there it is.

She felt I did not like her and soon left.

In an atmosphere of restored peace, we waited for Ashraf, who appeared before long, his round face still a trifle grey through its shiny black as a result of the illness of the bullet. He promised me that I should find my lodging in Baghdad, and gave me a letter to a friend of his who was to provide me with all I could possibly wish for. And so, full of hope, I set forth.

In the Moslem Quarter

To awaken quite alone in a strange town is one of the pleasantest sensations in the world. You are surrounded by adventure. You have no idea of what is in store for you, but you will, if you are wise and know the art of travel, let yourself go on the stream of the unknown and accept whatever comes in the spirit in which the gods may offer it. For this reason your customary thoughts, all except the rarest of your friends, even most of your luggage—everything, in fact, which belongs to your everyday life, is merely a hindrance. The tourist travels in his own atmosphere like a snail in his shell and stands, as it were, on his own perambulating doorstep to look at the continents of the world. But if you discard all this, and sally forth with a leisurely and a blank mind, there is no knowing what may not happen to you.

For this reason I sent off only one of my letters of introduction—and that was to the friend of the Damascus tanner—and wandered out the morning after my arrival in Baghdad to find a house.

What you first see of the Caliphs' city is a most sordid aspect; a long low straight street, a dingy hybrid between East and West, with the unattractiveness of both. The crowd looks unhealthy and sallow, the children are pitiful, the shops are ineffective compromises with Europe; and the dust is wicked, for it turns to blood-poisoning at the slightest opportunity, and bears out the old Babylonian idea of an atmosphere inhabited by Demons.

But you can soon leave the main street and walk into the long bazaars and their twilight; or you can turn to the right

among the narrow ways and lattice-work balconies of the
Jewish and Moslem quarters; or better still, you can cross the
old bridge of boats to Karkh, which was the southern suburb
of the Round City built by Mansur, where the produce of the
land, once coming in great boats down the 'Isa canal, had to
unload into barges at the port near the ruin of Aqqar Kuf
where now is desert, since the masts of the ships could not
pass under the many stone bridges of the town.

The glory has departed, but the life is unchanged.

White-turbaned Indians, Jewish and Armenian merchants,
are still here, though their silks and spices, their indigo and
pepper, the sugar and velvets of Khuzistan no longer take the
old Aleppo road. Persian pilgrims or their descendants still
walk with silent bare feet and long fanatic faces through the
shadows of the dark and airless ways; and the sons of the
Prophet in green turbans, with flowing gowns and brown
rosary, still pass in grave abstraction, able no doubt to split
hairs in Tradition or Grammar, though the Mustanseriya, the
great college, is filled with the bales of the custom houses, and
the old disputes which rent the lives of men, the Creation of
the Quran or its Eternal Existence, have now given place to
the cheerful badinage of Kurdish porters under those carved
arcades.

I did not, of course, find all this out that very morning.

In fact I soon got lost in a labyrinth of ways so narrow that
donkeys with panniers filled them from side to side. I was just
thinking of enquiring the road home when I saw an empty
house.

It was a tumbledown-looking place, with brick walls and
grated windows evidently looking on to a small yard, and
there was an Arabic notice to say that it was empty and for
sale. But what attracted me was the house next door.

There, in a little garden court sitting under a shed on rows
of matting, were twenty or thirty children learning their lessons from an old Mulla who sat cross-legged among them.

They had only about ten books between them, so they sat in groups, three or four round each volume, and chanted the holy words in their childish voices. Now and then a little newcomer would pass me at the gate, slip off his shoes, and find an empty place and a corner of a book to read from. Now and then some of them got bored, strolled away among the plants and flowers, and returned after a while with renewed energy. The Mulla had a white turban and red hennaed beard, and a kind old face: his scholars evidently had no fear of him. It was such a pleasant sight, and I thought it would be so delightful to live next door to it, that I accepted the unnecessary assistance of five passers-by to decipher the address of the owner of the house, and made my way back to the depressing atmosphere of my hotel with a feeling of wonderful elation.

Very soon after lunch, Nuri Fulan, the tanner's friend, was announced. The letter, which was addressed merely "Baghdad," had reached him with this remarkable rapidity. How they do it in large Eastern cities is always a mystery to me: all the explanation I got this time was that there was an "acquaintance" in the post office.

One always expects one's friend's friends to be like them: what I imagined was an elderly Indian in long robes. Nuri, however, was a tall young man with the long Persian type of face, with a fine claret-coloured tie and European clothes, and the sort of forage cap which His Majesty King Faisal has chosen as the national headgear of Iraq. He was most encouraging and enthusiastic and very kind. Of course I could get a house for 1s. 6d. a day if I wanted it. He took my address of the morning, promised to look it up, and to arrange, if not for that one, then for another just as good. And he kept his word.

In a few days he had found me the smallest house I have ever seen and with the steepest and narrowest stairway. The street it stood in was only six feet wide, round two dark corners from the main street, and the house adorned it with a handsome door of varnished wood picked out with light blue paint and brass knobs and knocker. Inside was a little dark well far too small to be a court, with a sort of alcove opposite the front door: that would be the kitchen: a table, a primus stove, and a "hub" or earthen jar for water would be all the furniture required there.

On the left of the front door, behind a partition wall, the stair climbed up more steeply than anything that is not mountaineering. In times of siege it would be excellent for pouring molten lead on the attack. The strategic position, however, was weak at the other end, where anyone might arrange a converging assault from the roofs on either side, my own roof being separated from them only by a palisade of corrugated iron very much askew. This had been put up from motives of modesty, but one's natural curiosity was provided for by a series of little eyeholes cut at intervals.

Between the roof and the kitchen was my apartment, two cubicles joined by an open bridge across the well below. The back room was gloomy, but the front one had three windows all painted light blue. Only the upper halves were glazed: the lower closed with iron shutters that let down, so that one could not have the window shut and also look out. But it was a cheerful little room all the same. It looked on to the street, the blacksmith, the grocer, and the butcher's shop below, and the little court of a mosque opposite with a blue-tiled doorway and a nebk tree that brushed my shutters. It was all newly whitewashed. And the rent came to 1*s*. 3*d*. a day.

I left it all in Nuri's hands, and after bargaining and counter-bargaining the matter was settled. I spent a morning in what is known as the thieves' bazaar, bought what little furniture was small enough for the house, saw it loaded on the back of a Kurdish porter, and walked with him sedately to the door of my new home, where the neighbours gathered together to promise me sympathy and assistance while I lived among them. They all seemed friendly and delightful. Only the Mulla, a wizened old Shi'a with a wall eye, looked on from a distance with a sour expression which I hoped was the natural cast of his features or possibly a lifelong practice of theology: I was most anxious to be friendly, since my water supply came from the tap in the courtyard of his mosque.

Marie the Armenian

If one lives in a slum in Baghdad, the servant problem is just as acute as anywhere else, though of rather a different nature. At first sight there appears to be a great variety to choose from. There are men, Indian, Moslem, Armenian, Assyrian or Kurdish. There are Assyrian or Armenian maids, and one can get little boys into whose religions I did not enter.

In practice I found it very difficult.

I had to refuse a handsome Kurd because the house was too small for him and me together: his head reached the second story as he stood inside my front door.

An American acquaintance lent me her small page called Suleyman, aged fourteen. He was to have ten rupees a month, his bath paid for on Fridays, and a woolly vest when the weather got colder. He came cheerfully, carrying his basket behind me. When we turned into my alley, however, his face fell: at the second corner it took on an expression of settled gloom: and when I pulled out my latchkey, a dangerous weapon over a foot long and very heavy, and opened the door of my abode, he gave one disconsolate look round, put his basket on the floor, sat on the lowest step of my ridiculous staircase, and burst into tears.

Being a resourceful imp, he soon pulled himself together, ran to the main street where the ragamuffins of Baghdad sit on the pavement and wait to carry parcels, and came back with a broad-faced young Arab friend of his, whom he evidently considered more suitable to my establishment. Having so provided for me, Suleyman vanished tactfully into space.

Mahmud was a charming boy, with a face like the full

moon, always smiling: but the elements of housekeeping were not in him. My English friends too, who in all this time were as kind and helpful as anyone could possibly be and with whom I was staying while these problems were being settled, thought it would be better to have a woman who could stay in the house at night.

So I engaged Marie the Armenian.

She was a dark, untidy, loquacious creature, with eyebrows pencilled to meet over her nose and a tattoo mark on her chin made by the Beduin who had carried her off as a small child in a raid or a massacre and sold her to a Moslem of Damascus. He kept her till she was twelve and then married her. He seems to have treated her kindly, and to have been fond of her, for when she escaped he followed her to Baghdad and was still sending messages at intervals to beg her to return. This, at least, was her account of the matter. When I engaged her, she had just run away from Abdulla the tailor, who dresses the ladies of Baghdad: he also had apparently done nothing to deserve the sudden desertion, but Marie was like that. And she wanted to live with one of her own sex, having—so she told me—the very lowest opinion of the other. In spite of this, and although I am not one of those women who can tell at a glance who is moral and who is not, I could not help gradually coming to the conclusion that Marie was really more fitted to be a vivandière than a lady's maid.

She had a passion for bright colours. She went about drably enough, in the shoddy European things which are swamping the East, dilapidated high heels and jerseys knitted in hideous browns and yellows: but in the little cubicle opposite to mine, in a square bundle in which were all her worldly possessions wrapped in the quilt on which she slept, she had a collection of every sort of gaudy material. Now and then she would open it, pull the things out one after the other, look at them with pathetic pride, and fold them carefully away again. In her friendless wandering life that bundle was the only thing to which she could attach any feeling of home.

She developed a tyrannic devotion to me which was not only embarrassing, but also gave an uncomfortable sense of instability, like the affections of a tiger. If I went out to dinner, I returned to find her plunged in gloom. She lived in extremes, always either excessively truculent or exceedingly humble, so that life among our Moslem neighbours was complicated far more than it need have been, and I was sometimes exasperated into feeling that the chief cause of Armenian atrocities must be the Armenians. "One day they will murder us," she would say, peering down at the harmless and friendly greengrocer below. She would flash out with her basket in the morning, flaunting the eight gold bracelets which were her only capital and on which she counted for a rainy day, casting glances and repartee right and left to the shopkeepers' assistants, and stepping with an added provocative jauntiness past the chairs where a little congregation of Elders always sat and contemplated at the corner of the street. They, with unblinking eyes fixed disapprovingly on her feet, no doubt thought of her as did Isaiah of the ladies of Jerusalem. They never greeted her or she them, though to me they would answer with their blessing of peace.

"One day they will murder me for these," Marie would say, coming back from the markets and shaking the twisted gold on her thin tattooed arms.

"Why not cover them up?" I suggested.

"Like a Moslem? I would not cover myself for those dogs. I shake my arms in their faces." But if anyone knocked after sunset, she would not dare open. She flew upstairs to the little bridge between our rooms and there, pulling a contraption that communicated with the front door by means of a string, waited in an advantageous position for whatever might appear.

I was, indeed, no little troubled at the general loudness of her ways among our decently secluded Muhammadans, and did my best to see that she carried on her household tasks indoors and with the door shut, instead of on the doorstep in the street. The blacksmith came out of his smithy one day to congratulate me on these efforts of propriety, which were apparently observed and applauded by the whole neighbourhood.

"She has no intellect. She is ignorant," he said. "She is a savage. She is Armenian."

With every crescendo, the little party which had gathered round nodded approval.

"We all say she is not adapted to one like you," said the greengrocer with the air of a judge.

An old woman in black, her veil over one side of her face and a copper water jar on her shoulder, assented vigorously. The opinion of the street was evidently unanimous.

But during the evening, when I felt it impossible to leave her in the damp below and she would sit and sew beside me, she told me about her strange neglected life: her childhood out of hearing of her own people, among the desert Beduin: her early faint memories of horror and hunger in the country north of Antioch: her feeling of injury and exile which the casual kindnesses of her masters had never even blunted. She had been left alone in the world, to snatch from it what she could. A child of violence, her hand against mankind. In her blind way she longed for affection and the lovelier things of the spirit: but she had been steeped too deeply in hatreds, had known too little of gentleness, to recognize them if they came. I felt that she had probably never known a woman she could trust or with whom she could feel the general sisterhood of women, and so, though her Arabic was excruciating, though she was really unattractive and did her best to make my quiet little house feel like a beleaguered fort among the enemy, I kept her with me till she went of her own accord.

Life in the Slum

I used to wake up in the morning, in my room in the Moslem quarter, and listen to the women bargaining below in Persian Arabic which I found hard to follow.

Every quarter and every sect in Baghdad has different ways of speech, and an old lady once told me that she could remember the time when a bride from the far side of the town was looked upon as a foreigner. I was far from being able to notice such subtleties, but I liked to lie in my campbed with the sunlight slanting on to me from above my blue shutters, and listen to the eloquence below; the w'Allahs and y'Allahs expended over quarter of a pound of meat; the latest event recounted to small groups with sudden dramatic lowering of the voices; the general interchange of all the news and gossip that could interest the little world of which our narrow alley was the main artery.

By the time Marie appeared with my breakfast the shop-keepers had set out their wares and arranged the shelves at the back of the alcoves in which they lived during the day; the heavy shutters—evidently first invented for times of civil tumult, they were so massive—had been taken down; and the blacksmith's small apprentice was adding to the cleanliness of his shop and the dustiness of the street by stroking down his floor with a few fronds of palm leaf.

Women were coming to the mosque for the daily supply of household water, carrying the slim-necked copper jars on one shoulder in their graceful barefoot walk. Water is laid on in Baghdad, but only a few wealthy inhabitants in our street had taps to their houses; we all went to the mosque, which luckily had no cistern for the washing of the faithful, into which Marie would doubtless have thrust our water jar to save time and trouble. She used to bring back enough for my bath on every day except Fridays, on which day the mosque was so entirely dedicated to godliness that its sister virtue had to be neglected.

The mosque was my nearest neighbour. Its roof was on a level with my room, and the street between us was, as I have said before, certainly not six feet wide. Cats used to spring across from it at night through my open window and startle me till I grew accustomed to their green eyes in the darkness by my bed.

Decently veiled by my curtains, I could watch the Mulla at his ironing or see him when he climbed at noon from the court below to call the people to their prayers. With his cracked old voice and sour face, he turned to the four quarters of the city, and the beautiful words floated from him through the sunlight, over the screened roofs and shadowy ways.

I used to wonder about his ironing, for the clothes which hung about him had been washed, if ever, a very long time ago, and looked as if they had not been ironed at all. The mystery was explained later. He was a tailor in his spare time, and he used the roof as a pressing room, which he shared with all the pigeons. His patience with these creatures was the only virtue I was able to observe in him, so I may as well mention it. The first sign of his coming would be the sobbing flutter of their wings as he advanced with a long pole, shooing them away from the shady corner where he put his table and the charcoal brazier with the irons. There was something quaint and pathetic in the sight of the old Mulla, so very ragged and sour, bending with such grim concentration over the vanities of other people's clothes.

The pigeons, having settled down a few yards from their first position, began to stroll about again with the utmost nonchalance, straddling from side to side like babies just able to walk, and following every movement of his with silly quick jerks of their neck and croonings. Presently they had again covered the whole surface of the roof. They pecked round his feet and strolled in their fat way between him and his brazier. Then he would cast upon them a look of hatred—or perhaps it was just his wall eye—and, taking up his long pole, would shoo them gently and ineffectively to the opposite corner of the roof. These manœuvres were repeated ten times or more in a morning.

Down in the court under the nebk tree he kept his school. It was not so cheerful as the one I had seen on my first morning in Baghdad, but it was pleasant to hear the children and to watch them scampering away when the lesson was over. By this time the morning's shopping had come to an end, the blacksmith and the greengrocer were sitting together in silent companionship over a qalian, and the butcher at the corner had put up his shutters.

Strolling packmen now came along, shouting the wares they carried on their heads on round trays. Bananas and dates, pickles, European cottons, manna from Mosul: if one waited long enough, there was hardly an accessory of life that did not pass one's doorstep. Now and then it was two strolling singers, or a Beduin woman with earrings and silver coins whom we had up to tell our fortunes in a mirror. We bought provisions as they came along, or added to the household furniture, although as a matter of fact my friend Nuri had seen to almost everything we required.

In the afternoon, after his day in the Public Works Department, he used to turn up with a kettle or a stove or whatever I thought was missing to my ménage, and would help me to put up curtains and so on, which his sisters had sewn for me. They all came to tea, fitted their flowing black garments into my tiny room, and admired all they could possibly find to admire, which was far more than most of my English friends were able to do.

I was indeed surrounded by great kindness, and was very happy in my doll's house in the slum. A feeling of friendliness pervaded the whole street. It made a delightful contrast with the Baghdad newspapers, whose articles were chiefly anti-British at that time. We did not bother about nationalisms, and as for religions, I found every sect very pleasant if the other sect were not standing by. And people were extraordinarily kind. A very few days after my arrival, the blacksmith sent a message to say that he would try to work his fire only when I was out, as the fumes came curling up into my room. I used to leave my latchkey, which it was impossible to carry in anything except a small portmanteau, with the greengrocer. This horrified Marie, but pleased the Moslems—he being a Shi'a—though it was not so great a sign of confidence as I imagined, since I discovered later that all latchkeys in the neighbourhood opened anybody's front door indiscriminately, and I could always borrow a neighbour's if Marie happened to have carried mine off. Everyone was amused at my surprise over this arrangement. "You cannot expect *every* door to have a different sort of key?" they said.

"But then why have a key at all?" said I: a revolutionary suggestion which they had never even thought of, for a key is always a key, whether it keeps your door locked or no. Mrs. Aleshine went on the same principle when she put on flannel underwear to be immersed in the Pacific.

In spite of its charms, I do not think that our street was really very respectable.

The lady in the house next door, instead of being modestly enclosed in lattice work, sat at her open window. So did I, for that matter. As we both projected half-way across the alley, we could watch each other at our embroidery, exchange smiles and a few remarks, and feel quite intimate, though we never crossed each other's doorstep. Respectable or no, the open window seemed more friendly than the carved eyelet holes upon the other side, through which Someone peered down from invisible twilight upon the passing world.

In the evening, in fact up to midnight or so, the street would be filled with whisperings, rustling of moving draperies, subdued laughter which was full of mystery and pretty to listen to but which, in a vague way, I thought sounded unusual in an Oriental town where people ought to be shut up in their houses.

After that the police began to rush about with their whistles. They fill Baghdad with extraordinary animation all through the small hours of the night. No burglar there need ever feel that he may be come upon unawares. On the other hand, the police do their best to keep honest householders awake. From street to street they whistle to each other like nightingales in a wood, only much louder. And I believe they whistled with especial vigour under my window, for I had paid the sergeant two rupees, apparently for this particular purpose.

The Making of a Nationalist

The greengrocer came up to me in the street one day and in the best manner of the Arabian Nights told me that a wealthy householder, having heard of my interest in the Arabic language, asked permission to call. He would like to give me lessons. He wished to make it clear that he did not desire to be paid. All I might do in return was to talk English to him occasionally.

This was too charming. I enquired about the householder, and heard that he had been a schoolmaster at Ba'quba, had inherited from an uncle, and now lived with his wife and family in my neighbourhood, attending to his property, which consisted of several houses round about. He was a most respectable man. The greengrocer, with his hand upon his heart, assured me I need have no fears. I had none, as a matter of fact. I invited them both to coffee next day.

The householder's name was Nasir Effendi. He was a middle-aged stoutish man with grizzled hair, and plump cheeks, straight nose, small shrewd eyes, and an expression of agreeable placidity. He was dressed up in European clothes which he moulded into curves. He sat on his chair very straight, supported as it were on his own solidity; and when he answered a question his mouth would purse itself together in an infantile engaging way, as if suppressing a smile which was in constant danger of escaping. He looked what he was, a kindly, peaceable, unambitious man.

After his first visit, he came nearly every afternoon.

He had *business* in the mornings, he said. It might have been all the Business of State from the way he said it. Actually, it was the superintending of two or three workmen who were mending a roof or something in his house. Having finished with them, he would stroll down a couple of hundred yards to my door with an air of Property and Leisure about him which did one good to see. All my street looked up with respect to watch it. He had the daily paper folded under his arm with his forage cap or sidara, and his latchkey, as long and as heavy, and in fact an exact duplicate of mine, in his hand. Having climbed to my room, smoked a cigarette, drunk a cup of coffee and exchanged the news of the day, he would open the paper out upon my table and lead me, with many halts and interruptions, through the Baghdad journalists' flowers of invective, chiefly directed against our British crimes.

It was the fashionable thing to be anti-British in Baghdad at that time.

To be anti-British made you successful either as a lawyer, a politician, or a journalist; you made an income, and you were a patriot as well, which is as near as one can get in politics to eating one's cake and having it: whereas if you were pro-British, you were slanged as a Betrayer by your own people, and treated as a Negligible Quantity by your foreign friends, who were too busy conciliating their opponents to be able to waste much time on their supporters.

Most of the British in Baghdad have a low opinion of lawyers, journalists, and politicians. I am not at all sure that there is a good deal to be said for the legend which excludes the former *ex officio* from Paradise. With our usual disinterestedness, however, we spare no effort in producing as many of them as we can; we make them out of the sons of desert shaikhs, of Jewish merchants, of landholders and officials—all people who might be friendly until we so educate them as to produce an Energy for which at present there is no sufficient outlet and which can find its only way of existence in political agitations. The young man in the Arabian Tales stumbled carelessly on unsuspected talismans and evoked a Jinn by mistake; he had some right to be surprised. But we set about it knowingly: we no longer encourage the scholars to sit at the feet of a philosopher and imbibe harmless wisdom: we aim at something more tangible; strange as it may seem, we actually *try* to produce lawyers and politicians and journalists. We have not really much choice in the matter: what we do not do ourselves, other people will now do for us, so great is the world's thirst for instruction. But meanwhile, having produced these people in great numbers, there is not nearly enough work for them all; they are born for the trouble of others as the sparks fly upward. It would be the same if we had chosen to produce, say, tobacconists. If there were only one customer to every five tobacconists there would be trouble, even though a tobacconist is not educated to be a nuisance in the same professional way as those others mentioned above. What is peculiar is that we appear to be surprised at this state of affairs. "How ungrateful," we say. "All these people educated by us, writing these horrid things about us." Muhammad with the viper was more reasonable, for he held that as it is its nature to bite, it should not be counted as a crime. But we, having with great labour thrust upon the East a rather low form of Western culture, look on with shocked amazement while two and two make four.

This has little to do with Nasir Effendi.

As my Arabic began gradually to soar beyond the simplicity of Reuter's telegrams into the tortuous recesses of the leading articles, Nasir would brush aside points of grammar which bored him infinitely, and would launch out into long expositions of the iniquity of governments, particularly ours. He did it with astonishing frankness and—as he luckily had no personal grievance to complain of—with perfect good humour. He was anti-British because it was the obvious thing to be; all his friends were so; the editors told him to be so; he was none of your independent thinkers: he was one of that great body which we call Public Opinion because it has no opinion at all: he echoed our unpopularity because we had allowed our unpopularity to be the fashionable cry; a few native articles in an opposite direction would have turned him round in the inside of a month.

Meanwhile he was against us, and told me so with a little twinkle which grew only more pronounced when I assured him of the blatant untruthfulness of his favourite papers. I never found out whether he really believed them, or whether his attitude towards us was not rather that of a child watching the tide as it demolishes the castle which itself had built with so much enthusiasm so very short a while ago: there he stands, the innocent remorseless one, with the little spade which had been used for the building in his hand, ready to help with an insidious slap when the disintegrating forces of nature really show themselves. Indeed it is the forces of nature, rather than that capricious one with the spade, that need attending to.

Nasir would tell me of the days in Baghdad when the British army was fighting its way up the Tigris, and everyone who was not a Turk longed for their arrival. The Turks had all the food. They sent loads of wheat to Asia Minor, and the civilian Arabs in the towns of Iraq had a hungry, anxious time.

Nasir had been forced into the Turkish army, and fought at Ctesiphon. He and his Arabs were in the front rank, and not at all anxious to fight in a cause which was not their own. The Turks behind and the British in front both meant business, however, and Nasir described the unpleasantness of being between the two. The Turks were brave, he said: they would stand up again and again to the enemy, regardless of cover: Nasir and his men, on the other hand, would try to lie low and let things go over them as much as possible: this want of enthusiasm caused them to be constantly in trouble, and they were always placed so that the Turkish guns could rake them at a moment's notice.

Then, when the British took over the country, Nasir became a schoolmaster at Ba'quba, and adopted European
clothes. He did not think much of them. "There is not an
Arab," said he one warm day, "who does not take refuge with
Allah from the discomfort of your socks." But it was a symbol
of the new order. He tried to compromise by wearing a collar
and no tie, observing with some truth that he could see no
usefulness in the latter garment: the Political Officer, however, said that it was better to be either all European or all
Asiatic in the matter of clothes: Nasir submitted to our peculiar views on masculine adornment as part of the new civilization.

In his own house he returned to the long white gown.

I called there one day on his wife, a frightened wild creature
with long plaits who sat timidly on one corner of the red
velvet divan, evidently unused to chairs, and too shy to utter
a word. Fatima, their little girl, leaned against her father's
knee with round eyes: he was devoted to her. All his domestic
instincts, which had intended him for a quiet and contented
life at home, found an outlet in little Fatima. His wife, whom
he had married as a child, was too elementary a creature to
help any man to feel domestic.

It was pathetic to see him trying to tidy the feminine litter
of the room; to see his own corner with one hard straightbacked chair, and his library kept in an old paraffin case
where in the evenings he grappled with textbooks on political
economy.

"How comfortable you are," he would say, looking round
the tiny room my English friends thought so deplorable. "I,
too, like a house well-arranged; but what can I do? That is a
woman's business, and our women—they do not know: they
do not want to know."

"Little by little," said I. "It takes three generations. It is
only the government of your country that can be learnt in a
couple of years, according to your papers."

Whereupon he would purse up his mouth with that engaging twinkle of his, and say as he pulled out his daily rag: "There is a long article against the English here. It says they will not teach us to fly aeroplanes." (This was some years ago now.) "They are afraid. But it is natural," he would add; for he was becoming distinctly more tolerant. "It is only politics."

Concerning Smells

True happiness, we consider, is incompatible with an inefficient drainage system. It is one of those points on which we differ most fundamentally from the East, where happiness and sanitation are not held to have any particular connection.

In spite of many efforts, Baghdad still remains triumphantly Eastern in this respect. It lies so low and in so flat a land that there is no possibility of draining anything anywhere. This is what makes it so depressing for Officers of Health and so amusing for people who like to study microbes.

Every house is built round a paved yard, large or small: in the middle of the yard is a trap-door, which does not usually fit extremely well: under that is a cistern where all the refuse waters go. The Sumerians used to bury their relatives under the dining-room floor close by, a thing which is no longer done.

My little court as time wore on seemed to smell more and more like a Sumerian ancestor. I used to lie awake and wonder about it at night, and admire the malignity of a smell which could lie dormant all day when one might escape it by going out, and leaped upon one as soon as one was safely imprisoned in one's bedroom. There was something of the Babylonian fiend about it. Indeed, I believe it was an infliction called up by the Mulla next door, who did not like infidels in his quarter. What could be more easy to one who knows the ropes than to call up a Smell from the Baghdad underworld? The only difficulty would be to choose which, for there is a great variety. This was a particularly wily one. It never appeared by day so that I was unable to prove its existence to my friends and neighbours: it never troubled Marie, who slept with her head in the very midst of it over our diminutive cistern-court: but it curled under or through my closed door, crept up to the corner where I lay trying to breathe the comparatively innocent air of the street, and had me at its mercy for the rest of the night. It left me with a sore throat every morning.

The diphtheria, however, was started by people who lived a most sanitary life at Rustum Farm, far from such slums as mine. That they should get it and not I was the sort of injustice which makes one wonder whether the gods really approve of prudence as much as people who give advice would like you to believe.

I got a lot of advice at this time. The variety of ways in which I might die appeared to be surprising. The mere mention of the Smell made people look at me as if I were dead already. It would get worse, they said, in winter: after rain, the accumulated smells of ages would rise in one solid mass and hang over the paved cistern-courts of my regrettable district. I would be marooned, for those little sideways would be so deep in mud that I should be unable to walk in and out to the civilization of New Street. It was, as a matter of fact, already beginning to get difficult, for people were mending their roofs in preparation for winter: this meant caulking them over with a mixture of straw and mud, very liquid, which was dumped in the street close to the house to be treated, and turned it for the time being into a sticky soup from wall to wall. The masons stood in it nearly to their knees, sending it up in little buckets as it was called for: the man above took it and slapped it down with a sad little chant that gave his work a cadence.

"Where is my loved one?" Down went the bucket.
"Where is my son?" Up it came again.
"Where are my brothers?"
"Where is my father?"

"Where is my dear one?"

"Where are my friends?"

After listening a while one felt as if all the world were lost or missing.

The traffic of the street, being mostly barefoot, went on cheerfully undisturbed.

Even without these obstacles and in dry weather, I was always rather careful to keep near the sides of my street. Like the courtyards on either hand, it had a sewage system of its own, but no trap-doors to close it: there were holes at intervals all down the middle, crumbling into darkness below: [1] some of them had a few stones to break the fall, but mostly they were black openings into whose depth I never investigated, but took it for granted that I might be swallowed like the steam roller in New Street, when that thoroughfare was being civilized years ago.

The steam roller and Baghdad must have found each other very surprising when they first met, but other more primitive forms of municipal effort were obviously at home and did excellent work. Donkeys, for instance. Every morning they came collecting yesterday's rubbish and carried it off in oozing panniers which it was difficult but most advisable not to brush against in passing.

When it rained, men paddled out with spades and built tiny soft sidewalks like dykes. It made one realize what "taking the wall" meant in the Middle Ages, for when two people met there, the outer one had either to turn back or step into the water. Most of the Arabs would naturally expect the woman to do this, but I always waited and found that they accepted my ideas of precedence very obligingly. These were poor people, mostly: our quarter, I have said before, was rather of the lower sort. On muddy days I envied them; they could paddle

---

[1] These have mostly been covered over by the exertions of the Baghdad municipality and the little streets, cool and shady, are now the pleasantest thoroughfares in Baghdad on a hot day.

about light-heartedly, while I and the few effendis with shoes on had to get from side to side of the larger lakes on the backs of Kurdish porters who ferried us across for twopence.

In spite of all this, I liked my slum. I had no thought of leaving it. But I went in a moment of weakness to the Municipality and asked if there was anything people could do in Baghdad about smells. There I met Mr. B., who was very kind and asked me where I lived. He looked troubled when I mentioned the address: he came that very day to see me.

It was the cheerful middle of the afternoon; my dingy little street was basking in repose; the Smell had hidden itself as usual; my tiny house looked its best, with the sun shining opposite in the branches of the nebk tree by the mosque; and the butcher's shop had closed its shutters. But in spite of this I knew that all was up.

Mr. B. gave one glance into the dank recess where the Sumerian grandfather must have been buried; one other look to the yard of the mosque where my water came from. "There is only one thing to be done," said he. "You had better leave as quickly as you can."

"That is quite impossible," I said. "This is the only place in Baghdad where I can lodge for one and threepence a day."

Mr. B. was very sympathetic. The British Civil Service thinks that ladies who travel in the East for fun are eccentric: it discourages as many as it can and bears the rest with patience. I, however, was being not eccentric but merely economical. Mr. B. gazed at my house with the sad look which comes to sanitary inspectors in Baghdad whom nothing can surprise any longer. "I'll find you something better than this," said he. And so he did.

Within a week I had moved to a new home.

A Chapter of Discord

My new home was a room in the house of Elias, the Carpenter, and his wife Najla. It was on the western side of the Tigris, with five windows looking across the river towards the old British Residency, now the Air Vice-Marshal's house, and the houses of South Gate: they stand along the dingy river shore in a tawny line above blank walls when the river is low; but their doors are flush with the swollen waters when they rise in spring.

My house stood among palm groves and little Arab mud hovels on the opposite bank. Tops of palm trees showed over its walls from gardens behind it. It had two lower rooms for summer, and two upper ones with windows to catch the sun; and across the yard were dark alcoves and passages where Najla squatted over the cooking with a primus and a brazier on the ground. She had long hennaed plaits, and a face still beautiful, though she thought no more about it: her two children whom she served like a slave, her husband when he came from the town in the evening, Asma the Kurdish sheepdog, and the chickens, kept her busy: and she soon added me to all these whom she delighted to work for, for she was of a most generous and affectionate heart. She and all her family had one of the upper rooms, and I the other; and we shared the two terraces that faced the river and the court.

Something happened to the weather on the day of my flitting. A low yellow cloud in the morning turned rapidly into a dust storm. As we crossed the bridge of boats its pontoons quivered with little white river-waves breaking around them: across the water the landscape had become invisible. Marie, sitting beside me in the arabana, watched with increasing gloom as we jolted beyond the noisy district of gramophones and shops towards the suburbs; while Nasir and Nuri, who had both volunteered to help, and sat among packages on the little front seat, told her with rather forced cheerfulness of the delights of life in the "country"—quite in vain. I was busy attending to my more fragile household goods, as they danced in their baskets with every lurch in the sandy tracks among the palms.

Najla opened the gate to us with her charming smile.

Marie, I thought innocently, would now be delighted to find a Christian friend.

But I had forgotten that one was a Syriac Catholic and the other an Armenian. Marie no sooner saw her than she rushed, so to speak, at her throat. "Never have I been," said she truculently, "in such a lonely melancholy place. If the Khatun had but spoken before I would have found something more suitable to her station."

Najla's manners are excellent, but if there is a last word to be said, she is not one to let the other person say it. "You—Armenian?" she asked; and managed to convey unutterable insults by such simple means.

After that there was little to be done. The two women and the Kurdish sheepdog held the middle of the floor. Nasir and Nuri, after various efforts as peacemakers, took their leave of me with pitying shrugs; and I myself, having attempted furnishing in vain, fled across the river and took refuge with English friends, feeling that Asia and its schisms were too much for me altogether.

Filled with bitterness at the thought of those early bishops whose disagreements at the Council of Chalcedon, or wherever it was, were responsible for my present discomforts, I made my way back after an interval. The dust storm still raged, my little boat rocked about on the Tigris, and the discussion indoors was still going on with unabated fierceness. But my looks of dismay brought a temporary lull: with only subdued mutterings, as of a thunderstorm whose mind is not made up, the two women helped to bring some order into the chaos, and by the time darkness fell a little oasis had been made. Then I looked to see the time, for I was, as it happened, dining out that night.

My two watches lay side by side on the dressing-table. The Spirit of Discord had penetrated their machinery also; one said 7.45 while the other said 6.30: like the Christian sects, they were ticking away perseveringly, obviously convinced that each was right. But my dinner was at eight, and half an hour's drive away. And no one in this neighbourhood possessed any other watch.

At this moment Marie came to say that she had lost all the keys. The wickedness of the Syriac Catholics, she was prepared to argue, was responsible for this as for most other troubles: but I had had enough of theology for the time being. Scraping together what I could in the way of evening clothes, I dressed in haste, climbed downstairs to the court where, by the light of a lantern, the two were still engaged in their ancestral war, brushed aside their imploring hands as they awoke to the fact that I was going out into the night, and slammed the door behind me. A little path, I knew, though I had not been along it, went on the river bank towards the lights and the clocks of Baghdad. As I stepped into total darkness, I felt myself seized in both arms by an Arab.

There are ladies whose fascinations are a constant worry to them when they travel. The most unsophisticated savage appears to fall in love at first sight. The Desert Chief no sooner sees them than he wishes to carry them off. As for me, being small and plain and quite insignificant, such dangers do not trouble me: unflattering as it may be, I wander about the East without being incommoded at all.

I thought, however, that this particular Arab might want my handbag on so very dark a night.

A Chapter of Discord

His object, as it happened, was merely to save my life; I was stepping over the edge into the river.

There is usually a lantern at this corner, but it had been blown in by the storm. The Tigris, empty of boats, was flowing in solitude and darkness below, not in the least like one of the Rivers of Eden. My rescuer held me by the arm and led me along what there was of a path, explaining its pitfalls in shouts between the gusts of wind. He was a railway employee, he said, and spent his nights patrolling this neighbourhood where there are depots: he was resting in the shelter of our gate when I stepped out to apparent suicide. Where was I going?

"Trying to go to dinner," I said. "And I must find out the time."

We had now left the region of utter darkness and turned inland, and he stopped under a lamp-post. He was a nice-looking man with black eyes and moustache under a flowing white kaffiyah. He drew aside his brown abba, opened a khaki coat, unbuttoned the neck of his long zibun or gown, and from the folds of the white shirt below drew out a red embroidered case with the button of which he struggled while I tried to be patient. Finally he pulled out a little flannel bag; inside this was a metal case which contained a watch. He studied it with an intent frown. "Two o'clock," he said unexpectedly. Arab time begins at sunset.

"By our time," said he, seeing that I looked doubtful, "it will be eight-thirty."

"Wallah," said I, "and I was invited for eight."

"Is that so?" He looked regretful and turned to his watch again. "It is now, I think, seven o'clock," said he. He was doing his best.

Distressed as I was, I could not help laughing, which puzzled him. "Let us make it seven-thirty," I suggested. "That will suit me better."

"Seven and a half," said he. "Good. It is possible." He put away his watch in its several cases with care and pride.

Near the Maude Bridge we found a clock but no cabs. The time was only seven-fifteen, and all was well. The dust had cleared and there were stars. The long and empty bridge of boats writhed and shook like a snake in the small white fangs of the stream. My escort took me across and left me. He would take no money; but he said he would come one day and ask me to write him a testimonial.

And so it was. One day he appeared with a big fish in his hand as a present, and I wrote out a testimonial and saw him fold it away with the watch and his amulet in the little red case round his neck. What he expected from it I was unable to discover, and he would take no other gift. I hope it may bring him luck.

The Life of the River

The width of the Tigris in Baghdad is about four hundred yards, a noble stream. It is the only sweet and fresh thoroughfare of the town: not clear water, but lion-coloured, like Tiber or Arno. Its broad flowing surface is dyed by the same earth of which the houses and minarets on its banks are built, so that all is one tawny harmony. Its low winter mists in early morning, or yellow slabs of sunset shallows when the water buffaloes come down to drink after the day; its many craft, evolved through the centuries so that one looks as it were upon an epitome of the history of ships from the earliest days of mankind; the barefoot traffic of its banks, where the women come with jars upon their shoulders and boatmen tow their vessels against the current: all this was a perpetual joy in my new home.

I used to watch the different vessels from my terrace. Gufas, bowl-like coracles of woven basket coated with pitch, with a blue bead or two and a few cowrie shells embedded for luck in the rim, floating down filled with sand or melons; the boatman with his square clumsy oar gives a skilful circular movement now and then to keep in midstream, as his fathers did before him when Nineveh was building.

Kalaks come down from Mosul, their planks and the inflated goatskins which support them hidden under a cargo of brushwood.

There are slender maheilas with pointed overhanging bows and sloping mast: long rectangular barges, called shahturs, you see in Assyrian sculptures: the smart launch of the High Commissioner: and little motor boats run by Arabs in ragged kaffiyahs who carry you for a few annas from point to point of the stream. Najla would stand on the bank and call: "Oh Father of the Motor, come": and the father of the motor, puffing by, would put out a plank to the soft mud and pick us up: more often, however, seeing that our number was small and unimportant, he would imitate the London bus driver and gaze into space in the opposite direction.

Sometimes steamers would bring American tourists for a week-end in Mesopotamia. And sometimes pilgrim steamers for the Holy Cities would come upstream, packed so that there was scarcely standing room, with black and green banners unfurled against the landscape of the shore: the "haussa" of the passengers—"Ya Hasan, ya Husein"—repeated over and over again with a fierce monotony and a sort of growl at the end of each beat, could be heard above the noise of the engines as this strange combination of the ages of Faith and Mechanics came round the eastern bend.

In winter mornings a low white mist hung over the river.

I used to be rowed across, and watched the domes and minarets gather, as it were, out of a dream,

"so faintly flushed, so phantom fair,"

their bases lost in vapour, their outline clear against a very pale sky, as my "bellum" lapped across the shrouded water towards the unseen shore.

Old Salih the boatman, dressed in a dingy shirt, a black and white kaffiyah of the Shi'as wrapped round his cunning, watery-eyed old face, looked up at me with a pious aphorism now and then as he rowed with humped shoulders. He usually had a trail of fish for market threaded on a cord and kicking out by the boat's side—a painful sight which made one think of that Persian King who kept his prisoners together by a rope run through their armpits. Kindness to fish did not enter into Salih's catalogue of merits, but he was great on fasting, which is a lucky virtue to be fond of if one is very poor. In Ramadhan he would meditate voluptuously on the punishments awaiting people who breakfast after sunrise in their houses.

He knew all the superstitions of the river: the Jinn, the Divs, the invocations to Elias who hovers on its shores at sunset. He knew the names of the stars: the Children of the Coffin, who follow the North Star to its eternal funeral; and Sirius and Betelgeux, the lovers, who are Majnun and Leila and meet, said he, together in the heavens on one night in the year.

He would sit humped on a corner of a wooden bench in the coffee house waiting for me when I came from a dinner party, or lie in his grey rags beside a lantern in the bottom of his boat where the river lisped through shadows at the end of a narrow lane. I thought little of this steep and dark way home over the cool night-water, but a surprised look used to appear on the faces of friends who saw me to the edge and left me in the hands of my rather disreputable-looking old Charon.

I had an affection for him. He was a gay old philosopher without any morals at all. He was always ready to gamble his four annas at the coffee house instead of saving them up for lunch. He finally disappeared owing to this weakness of his and to my own heedlessness.

As we drew near the end of Ramadhan he asked me one morning for ten rupees to buy his son a new gown on the feast day. The son was a blear-eyed little creature with close-cropped hair and a skull-cap, a sort of spawn of the river, born in a mud hovel on its banks, brought up in the mud and water of its shores, with an amphibian intelligence that would never rise above that slimy level. His cunning little eyes and those of his father fixed me with anxious calculation while I debated the matter of the rupees. They would row me across, said Salih, for *nothing* till the sum was made up. "Wallah, Khatun, it is hard if one's son has not something new for the Feast." In a moment of weakness I agreed.

Salih has never more been seen on our bit of the river. He

took away his boat but left his wife behind him. He also gathered all the fish he could collect from various friends, promised to sell them in the market, and added the proceeds to his loot. We heard of him, for he had moved only a mile or so upstream, but to all intents and purposes it was as if he had removed himself into space.

I tried to think better of him for three days. Then my thoughts turned to the police. As everyone knew where the old scamp was to be found, it seemed to me a fairly simple matter. I asked advice of my new boatman, Husein.

Husein hesitated. "Perhaps it would be as well if the Khatun were to say nothing about it," he ventured at last. "When the Khatun gave those ten rupees to Salih, he happened to have his boat near the Polis Station. He and the Polis played for the ten rupees, and the Polis won. I do not think the Khatun will find the rupees again."

A Visit in the Desert

"Would you like to visit my cousin, Shaikh Habib of the 'Azza?" said Nasir Effendi one day.

It is difficult to believe, when looking at Nasir's comfortable figure and city appearance, that he has anything so primitive as a Beduin cousin, but this is the manner of the East, where all holds together in the most intimate and unexpected way. I said I should be delighted, and, being still new to Baghdad and unaware of its peculiar attitude towards the female tourist, began to ask which of my English friends would like to join me.

This caused pain all round.

A document was handed to me,[1] printed for the guidance of ladies in Iraq and advising them, if they must wander, at least not to do so by themselves. "Ladies," it proceeded to say in language elegant but cautious, "are *deemed* to be accompanied when travelling with a European or American of the male sex."

This seemed to me an indelicate suggestion on the part of the British Civil Service with which it was unnecessary and hardly respectable to comply.

The next step, however, was even more crushing. "If you get into trouble by doing this sort of thing, no other woman will ever be allowed to do it afterwards," was one of those remarks which one can ponder over for hours without getting to the bottom of. An uncle of mine never allowed his hair to grow because he said that to keep it shaved prevented it from

[1] See page 49.

falling out: this was the same principle of prudence: but the sad moral came towards the end of his life, when he decided to give his locks their one fling, and nothing was left but baldness. I did not mention this instructive case to my friends.

The younger women were not unsympathetic: a gleam of adventure came into their eyes, which only made me unpopular with their husbands. A husband in an official position is like a Victorian débutante: a mere nothing blasts his career for ever. Apart from this, husbands in Services are expected to act as anchors when stray currents threaten to sweep their wives away, and the business of an anchor is, after all, to become unresponsive and spiky whenever one pulls at it. I began to feel like a Disturber of the Peace. This morbid nervousness about the doings of women when left to themselves could only be accounted for, I concluded, by the fact that Baghdad is near the site of the Garden of Eden: it must be a case of subconscious shock in the past. I began to feel like an anomaly: so many different people disapproved of me all at once, it might look as if I, and not they, were peculiar—which was absurd. I thought, rather bitterly, that if Paradise were run by the Colonial Office, there would be no chance of getting in at all, and felt thankful that in all probability it is not. I then went and told my woes to S., who instantly and gallantly said she would come, and would mention it to her husband—the most tolerant of anchors as a matter of fact—next morning at breakfast just before we started, when remonstrance would make him late for his office.

After this all sorts of risks and emotions might reasonably have been expected, but the rest of my diary is one continual anti-climax. Nothing showed the least sign of happening except the weather. We started off in the Solitude deplored in the printed definition, but otherwise and in our own minds rather tightly packed and crowded, what with Nasir, an Arab driver, a Jewish proprietor, and our food and bedding in a small but antique car. The Shaikh had gone ahead to prepare our reception.

We made north-east towards the Jebel Hamrin, through Ba'quba and Daltawa. The weather, as unencouraging as the remarks we left behind us, lay about in a thick white mist, most unusual and perverse. We took the desert with us, as it were, travelling in a small yellow patch surrounded by whiteness on all sides. The brambles were wet, the mist hung in festoons in the palm gardens of Daltawa, opening to show fronds here and there, high up as in cathedral aisles: the garden lanes between mud walls were silent: the gates, with wooden locks whose enormous bolts slide pegs into holes and are as clumsy and ingenious as any Eastern contrivance—were all fast closed: and near the village the mud became so bad that, after getting out of our car and watching its corkscrew wriggles, we insisted on having the chains put on.

After Daltawa the mist lifted; the desert appeared with sharp outlines under a watery sky. But the harm was done and every little hollow was a trap for motor cars. Our Arab drove slowly up and down the edge of the sticky streaks looking for a crossing place; he dashed at it full speed; there was a grinding noise in the middle; and after a quivering effort to grip earth that had the consistency of toothpaste, our car slid gently back while its wheels went round like fireworks, shooting water instead of sparks. Then we would get out and push, while the Arab driver used methods of persuasion with his gears: the Jewish proprietor was too well dressed to help us, but he stood in front and beckoned to our car with one finger, as if it were a baby.

We had just got out of our second ditch of this kind when we became aware of two Kurdish Members of Parliament, stuck in the mud more deeply than we had been, and in terror of their lives in the desert. Our united efforts had no effect at all on the magnificent saloon in which they travelled for their country's good, but as we were regretfully abandoning them, we saw help coming in the shape of three or four Beduin striding out of the mist towards us. We pointed them out, rejoicing, and apparently added the last strain to the already harassed feelings of the marooned politicians. "Do not leave us to the Beduin," they implored, as if it were a matter of certain death. We however, like greater powers before us, felt rather bored with the Safeguarding of Minorities—and the Beduin looked very peaceful: we left in a pathetic silence, but enquired about the fate of the deserted ones on our way back next day and heard that they had been rescued in the most uneventful manner—another anti-climax.

The mist now rolled into clouds and fled, casting shadows under the sun, and the desert in the direction of Dali Abbas began to show cultivation and to become more solid underfoot: and when, long after our expected time, we reached the first cornland, a messenger from Shaikh Habib stood up to meet us, a dark-skinned, aquiline-faced, black-bearded figure dressed in white, whose fierce appearance would have made the Members of Parliament faint away altogether.

Crouching on the footboard, he guided us, with a sense denied to the town-bred driver, in and out of irrigation ditches to the mud village where the Shaikh and his people are leaving their nomad habits and settling on the land: they are in the early stages of the process and still look upon houses as scarcely more permanent than tents, things to be left and built up again somewhere else if for any reason, such as a dispute with the tax collector or difficulty over grazing or irrigation, the site becomes distasteful. Shaikh Habib was thinking of doing this soon, he explained, because of some business with rents. Followed by a little group of tribesmen, he took us round the village, on a mound whose gentle regular rise showed that it had probably been inhabited off and on since Babylonian days.

All here was a mixture of new things and very old. The

A Visit in the Desert

Shaikh himself was such. Dressed in a yellow and black striped gown, or zibun, with a knife in his sash, and sleeves which ruffled over his hands, long and delicate as Van Dyck might have painted—a trait, by the way, often noticeable among the Beduin chiefs—he talked to us about the League of Nations, about his new school with French educational posters on its mud walls, and about raids in the neighbouring hills—a matter, he explained, of the past. His vegetable garden, with marigolds growing up among the cabbages, was a novelty to the tribe: but close by this sign of progress, in a room darkened so that her eyes might not be tired by the incessant turning, a young girl ground corn between two stones. The upper one had a hole into which a stick was thrust to make a handle to turn by. As she sat crooning an endless little song over that weary mill, one realized why this has ever been the labour of captives, a sad monotonous labour. How many mournful thoughts, how many dear and bitter memories, must have hovered over such grinding stones, from the days of Kassandra in the house of Agamemnon to those of our own women in Cawnpore.

We stood a while on the mound watching seven gazelles flashing away in the distance at great speed, their light hindquarters making them visible in the sun. Then we turned out of the cold air into the Shaikh's hall and sat among the tribesmen in a half-circle round a fireplace piled high with sesame-plants and thorns, watching their faces in the flamelight and listening to the rebaba, the one-stringed ancestor of the fiddle, as it played one or other of their four modes of music, for love and war and tenderness and sorrow, as they say.

During the rising in 1920 Shaikh Habib sheltered a British officer and apparently acquired some useful knowledge, for before dinner was brought in, he got up with an air of secrecy and asked us to accompany him to our room; here, spread on a ledge which corresponded to a toilet table, we saw two glasses and four bottles: burgundy, whisky, brandy and crême de menthe, as far as I can remember. "I do not like to have them out in front of the tribesmen," said our host, "but I know this is what you are accustomed to." He prepared to stand by and watch us. We, however, assured him that the national standard is lower for women and, much touched by his thoughtfulness, returned to the hall to eat the most enormous and delicious dinner I can remember for a long time.

We went to call on the Shaikh's wife after dinner, and had an experience, for we saw real beauty—not the kind that depends for its charm on some combination or accident of light and expression, but beauty absolute in itself and satisfying. She was draped in black so that only her face showed—oval, delicately pointed at the chin, with eyebrows gently and regularly curved over her great eyes. The features were perfect; she was not dark-skinned, but very pale; and very shy, so that she would hardly speak; and in the dim room, in her black gown, with her quiet way and queenly loveliness, she might have been Proserpine imprisoned in the realms of night.

There *was* a prisoner in the room, as a matter of fact; but she, as is the contradictory way of things, did not look like one, and sat on the ground hung round with every conceivable bead and jewel. She was an Armenian bought by Shaikh Habib at the time of the massacres, and evidently happy in her master's home, where she had been brought up, and presented with a husband and with all the trinkets that adorned her. There are many of these Armenians among the tribes of Northern Syria and Iraq, and they do not seem to be unkindly treated; but I remember one such among the Shammar who had not lost her sorrow through all these years, and would sit and weep day after day in her husband's tent (for she had been married to quite a well-to-do man among them); and when we stayed there she begged us for news of her people, of whom she had heard no word since the forced separation on the Nisibin road in her childhood.

This was the last of our stay with Shaikh Habib. We retired

to rest with one of his men stretched across the outside of our threshold to guard us through the night, and next morning, reluctant but threatened by rain, and with the potential remarks of Authority loud in our consciences, returned by the Khalis canal to Baghdad.

Note 1. See page 43.

EUROPEAN AND AMERICAN LADIES IN IRAQ.

REGULATIONS REGARDING RESIDENCE AND TRAVELLING.

An Administrative Order just issued states:

1.—GENERAL.

(i) The grant of visas to European and American ladies and ladies of similar national and social status for Iraq is subject to the following instructions defining procedure as regards residence and movements.

(ii) Ladies who do not comply with these instructions render themselves liable to the cancellation of their visas.

2.—RESIDENCE.

(i) Instructions may be issued from time to time specifying places at which European and American ladies and ladies of similar national and social status may reside without special permission.

(ii) From the date of coming into force of these instructions the cities of Baghdad, Basrah and Mosul are placed in this category but in respect of all other places a special "Residence Permit" must be obtained from the Minister of Interior.

3.—MOVEMENTS.

(i) *Definition.*—(*a*) By "local authority" is meant the Mutasarrif of the Liwa concerned, and in his absence the Commandant of Police.

(*b*) A lady is said to be "accompanied" when one European or American member of a similar national and social status of the male sex is travelling with her.

(ii) *Rules General.*—Ladies wishing to travel unaccompanied outside any of the cities referred to in para. 2 (ii) should (*a*) obtain the previous sanction of the local authority of the Liwas which they intend to visit; (*b*) arrange that all journeys by road are performed between sunrise and sunset and (*c*) keep to the main roads unless they have obtained the specific sanction of the local authority to do otherwise.

(iii) Ladies accompanied may travel on any of the main roads outside the cities referred to in para. (ii) without special permission with the exception of the special areas for which special rules are defined in para. 3 (iv), subject to the journey being performed between sunrise and sunset.

(iv) *Special Rules for Special Areas.*—

(a) Kerbala and Najaf.—

Ladies wishing to proceed accompanied or unaccompanied to the Kerbala Liwa (i.e., the Holy Cities of Kerbala or Najaf) must first obtain written permission from the Ministry of Interior. Applications can be made to the Assistant Director-General to the Ministry of Interior at the Serai, Baghdad.

(b) Arbil Liwa.—

Ladies, whether accompanied or unaccompanied, require special permission from the local authority for travel within the Liwa.

(c) Kirkuk Liwa.—

Ladies accompanied may travel without restriction on any of the car roads in the Liwa. If travelling unaccompanied they must first consult and get the permission of the local authority.

(d) Mosul Liwa.—

Ladies accompanied may visit Mosul town without special permission. They may enter the Mosul Liwa from Baghdad either via Baiji or via Guwair or Makhlat. Whether accompanied or unaccompanied they must obtain the previous permission of the local authority before visiting Tal Kaif, Tal Uskof, Al Qosh, Zakho, Ain Sifni, Shaikh Adi, Tal 'Afar, Sinjar, Hatra, Aqra, Amadia, and Ser Amadia. All journeys to Hatra must be made direct from Mosul. Two cars are necessary and a police escort must be taken. They must also obtain the permission of the local authority before proceeding by the trans-desert routes from Mosul to Syria.

(e) Sulaimani Liwa.—

Ladies, whether accompanied or unaccompanied, proceeding to Sulaimani or Halabja, must ensure that the local authority is aware of their intention and the time of their departure. They must arrange beforehand for their accommodation in both places.

4.—CAMPING.

Ladies, whether accompanied or unaccompanied, should give notice to the local authority of their intention to camp out at night and should be guided by the advice given.

5.—ESCORTS.

Ladies are warned that in some cases the local authority require that a police escort should accompany them—such escort can be supplied at their expense.

6.—EXCEPTIONS.

These instructions do not apply to passengers travelling on the Kirkuk—Nisibin Railway Convoys, or by recognized cross-desert transport companies plying between Baghdad and Syria.

Minister of Interior.

NOTE.—For the convenience of travellers in Baghdad, applications under these rules may be made direct to the Assistant Director-General of the Ministry of Interior.

Note 1. See page 43.

A Letter to the Baghdad Times.

_____

THE SOCIAL STATUS OF LADIES.

A PROBLEM FOR THE AUTHORITIES.

To the Editor.

Sir,—In your paper of Oct. 18th you give a detailed though possibly not a comprehensive list (for that would be beyond any human ingenuity) of things that Ladies in Iraq are not supposed to do.

As an earnest and interested enquirer, may I ask for a few further details?

What, exactly, is meant by a "Similar Social Status"?

It is quite difficult enough, in these days, to define a "Lady," but when she has to have a Similar Social Status as well, it becomes impossible without the help of some lucid official definition.

It is rather important, for I gather from the above-mentioned document that if she is neither a Lady, nor pos-

[52]

A Visit in the Desert

sessed of any Social Status in particular, the authorities do not really mind what becomes of her, and she may pic-nic off the main road without notifying the Ministry of Interior.

I take it that before accepting any invitation that may be made, she must also be very careful to look into the adequate Social Status of the European or American who is to accompany her. This is always judicious, especially when travelling abroad—and cannot be too carefully recommended. But a few hints as to how to decide on such a matter at short notice, would be very useful. Socks and ties and an Oxford manner are apt to be misleading, and a short test that could be applied rapidly whenever any excursion or expedition is under discussion, appears to be highly advisable.

As to main roads—they are not always recognizable in this country. They suddenly turn into a flat desert and one finds that one is off them. Under such circumstances, is a real lady, with Social Status and all, liable to have her visa cancelled?

Yours,

ENQUIRER.

Concerning Manners

If a Frenchman were to talk in his light-hearted way about either God or the Devil at a British dinner party, he would immediately discover that a knowledge of the English language is not enough in itself to make conversation easy.

Every country has its own way of saying things. The important point is that which lies *behind* people's words, and the art of discovering what this is may be considered as a further step in the learning of languages, of which grammar and syntax are only the beginning. But if we listen to words merely, and give to them our own habitual values, we are bound to go astray.

The Eastern values are particularly different from ours, and the traditions from which they derive belong only remotely to our group of traditions: the learning of them is a long affair. Englishmen have to spend much time over it, and have a wide range of people in their daily jobs from whom to gain experience: but to Englishwomen it is a matter of time and trouble which does not come naturally into the day's work, and which they therefore rarely undertake. They sometimes try, with insufficient knowledge on both sides, to make native friends; and it is an unsatisfactory business in every way, when the simplest object means one thing to one and something quite different to the other.

It is a pity. To know the machinery of other sorts of minds always makes life amusing, and in this case it is worth some effort on other grounds as well.

Many Englishwomen spend the best part of their lives in the East; they have opportunities to know and influence people of all kinds; in fact, whether they wish it or not, to influence them, for good or ill. They are two-edged instrument in the hands of Empire since no other women live their lives abro way—but also a dangerous one, for it is never always unconsciously working either for or against us. And since we are not now so popular as we once used to be, and are rather in need of as much goodwill as we can conveniently find among our neighbours, it seems a pity that women who slave away at home at committee meetings, district visiting, local government, and all sorts of meritorious but not amusing things, should grudge time and effort and, let us say it, a good many hours of boredom, to the understanding of what lies around them abroad.

A dreadful conclusion is forced on one as one travels. The British appear to be popular wherever they go until they come to settle with their wives.

The mere fact that such an importation makes the home more pleasant than it was causes an exclusion, though an unavoidable one, of the outer world. It creates a barrier which was not there before they came.

If to this they add complete ignorance, and the strange conviction that to be interested in things around one is in bad taste and almost immoral—then there is no limit to the harm they can do. It is much easier for most people to forgive a real injury rather than a slight to their vanity, and a want of interest is the most insidious way of hurting their feelings. It is all the more stupid if it is done unconsciously as is usually the case. In fact, when living abroad, especially, it is always as well to remember the definition of a gentleman as someone who is never *unintentionally* rude.

An illustration of this regrettable matter brought about the end of my friendship with Nasir Effendi.

Nasir Effendi found my removal to Najla's house across the river rather a trial. He could no longer stroll down after lunch

.vith his paper and his latchkey under his arm; it meant half an hour and four annas to a boatman whenever he came to see me. He did come on Mondays, however, and used to sit and argue about the iniquities of the British in a way that grew more and more tolerant as time went on. Nuri, who also came on that day, was as emphatic on the other side, and Najla and I attended to the coffee.

On this particular day, however, we happened to be leaving the British Empire to deal alone with its own enigmas. We sat at ease. Nasir, his figure a perfect harmony of contented curves, sat in the best chair; Nuri's long black-browed face was silhouetted against the window and the Tigris, when Mrs. X. came to call.

Mrs. X. is a kind woman and this was her first (and last) call. She came prepared to be kind, in spite of the difficulties of dealing with the social position of people who live in native houses. But the sight of my two visitors was unexpected. She stiffened ever so slightly—imperceptibly to any but people who are on the look-out for it. The Westernized Eastern is permanently on the look-out for it, which makes intercourse even more difficult than it need be. I felt at once that the afternoon was going to be a failure.

The visible shock was over in a second, however. I made the introductions. Nuri, delighted with the chance of a new European to talk to, was amiable. Nasir was on the defensive, though Mrs. X. did not know it. She herself was polite.

Unlike other races, we are bad at politeness unless we happen to like people. Mrs. X. may have tried, but she failed. If she had made one humanly friendly remark, even about the weather, even after that unfortunate beginning—she and I and the British in general would not have made an extra enemy that day. A very small crumb of interest would have sufficed. What she did was to look straight before her as if the gentlemen on either hand had become suddenly invisible and disembodied. She looked at me and talked to me: they might have been sitting in the moon, and that is no doubt what they felt like, for the atmosphere was cold. Presently Najla brought tea. Najla, prepared to smile upon the new lady and recount my virtues—an infliction which she always managed to draw out to great length for favoured visitors—saw that the occasion was not auspicious and retired to her room. Nuri talked. He took the opportunity to tell Mrs. X. that her husband was a good man and that all Baghdad thought him so. Mrs. X. evidently felt she could find this out for herself. Instead of being pleased, she considered Nuri an interfering insect, but tried not to show it: she looked at him with a faint surprise not intended to be offensive, and changed the subject. Nuri luckily had been fortunate in earlier contacts with the British and did not take the *nuance* as a sign of national malevolence. But he felt that we were not enjoying ourselves, and soon took his leave.

Not so Nasir Effendi. If the Superior Englishwoman desired his absence, she was not going to get it. He sat limp but immovable in his chair, in irritating silence.

And he won. After a decent interval of conversation like an Arctic Ocean, with remarks like icebergs floating about, few and far between—Mrs. X. took her leave. I saw her down the steps. She was quite unaware of having awakened hatred in the heart of a peaceful citizen.

When I returned, Nasir fixed me with real malignity in his little placid eyes. "I knew she wanted me to go," he said. "I could see what she was thinking. They call us wogs." He put his cup down with a bang.

"It was unfortunate," I admitted. "But you are rather unjust if you think she meant to insult you. You have no idea how rude we are to each other, and think nothing of it. It is just a habit of ours. It is almost a sign of friendliness. You hold that courteous speeches are necessary; we suspect them: we are always afraid that if one is polite one must be a liar. And if you had ever lived in the country of England," said I, knowing it was useless but enjoying his surprised expression, "you would know that the most fantastic things are possible. People who have lived there for years scarcely speak to each other when they meet, unless they have an introduction from the Prophet himself or at least from one of the Imams of the County."

Nasir looked at me with round eyes. It was no good. He did not believe me. I really had nothing to do with it, but he never came to see me again.

A Syriac Christmas

Najla, my landlady, and Elias the carpenter, were Syriac
Christians from Diarbekr, and belonged to that part of the
sect which Rome has gathered into its fold, without altering
many of the old customs and ritual. Near Christmas time
Najla told me that they were going to read the Gospel out in
the court by a bonfire on Christmas Eve, as every family
does—and would I join in the ceremony?

I was going out that evening, and dressed a little earlier, and
found the two small boys, Yusuf and Charles, waiting on my
doorstep, their feelings equally divided between the splendour
of my appearance in evening dress and the excitement of a
bonfire. They took me one by each hand into the open court,
where small lanterns were hanging among red and green paper streamers, and a heap of dry thorns stood in one corner.

"The youngest should read, but Charles knows only his
ABC," said Najla while she handed us candles, "so it will
have to be Yusuf. May the Holy Words bring you all your
heart's desire, oh light of my eyes." She kissed me, and after
her the two children came up shyly and lifted their cheeks to
be kissed, while Elias, his tarbush pushed back off his grizzled
old aquiline face, smiled upon us all.

Then Yusuf, who is ten, read out the Gospel. He stood very
straight with the lighted candle in his hand, his face full of
seriousness, an impressive little figure under the stars. There
was no wind; the candle flames burned clear and still. The
four walls shut out everything except the motionless tops of
the palm trees in surrounding groves. The outer gate was
locked and barred, in memory, no doubt, of many persecu-

tions. In the childish Arabic, the old story came with a new and homely grace; and we listened, moved and silent, standing like living altars, holding our lighted candles. When it was over, Elias bent down with a match to the fire; the children clutched my arm in excitement. "Watch how it burns," said Najla; for the luck of the house depends on it. The match went out.

Elias tried again; a little flame flickered and hesitated; Najla, resourceful, contradicting the tenets of Predestination, poured paraffin on the strategic point, and the fire leaped to a blaze. It lit the children's oval faces with their long, dark lashes, and Najla's hennaed plaits with kerchief tied above them. The four voices joined in some old native psalm; and the flame of the fire, rising so straight into the quiet sky, made one think of yet earlier worships, of Abel and Abraham and Isaac; and older than these, for presently, when the thorns were but red embers, Najla took my hand and made me leap thrice across them, wishing my wish, as no doubt the Babylonian maidens did to the honour of their gods.

Next morning, at 4.30 a.m., when the minarets across the water scarce showed against the faintness of the dawn, my hostess and I were already on our way to Mass in the Syriac Church. The bridge of boats was deserted. The sentry, evidently a Christian also, gave Najla palpitations by informing her that we should be late. Najla keeps her high heels and her walking for great occasions only, and they were a little unmanageable.

We reached the Christian quarter across the early silence of New Street, and found its dark alleys filled with quiet streams of people on their way to the Chaldean, Armenian, Latin, Syriac, or Jacobite churches, which are all hidden away unobtrusively among the labyrinth of houses. They are modern and ugly when seen in the vacant light of day, but now, as we came from the half-light outside, we opened the heavy door on what looked like a bed of tulips brilliantly illuminated, so vivid and rustling and shimmering were the many-coloured silk *izars* of the women who filled the nave in the light of lamps and candles.

In the centre of the church, half hidden by the crowd, the Bishop and his clergy were busy over another bonfire, surrounded by men who chanted a wild swift Syriac hymn—the tongue in which legend says that Adam lamented over the death of Abel. The male congregation at the back kept up the humming monotone accompaniment which takes the place of an organ.

As we entered, the dry wood caught fire and a sheet of flame rose half-way to the ceiling. The silken hoods round us rustled like a field of barley in a breeze. The Bishop, in a robe of cream and gold and crimson, his mitre high above the congregation, took in his arms a figure of the Infant Christ on a crimson cushion. Followed by his train, he walked slowly round the church, while a low canticle, wild no longer, but deep and grave and very touching, rose from all sides where the men were standing. The women did not sing.

After this the service continued very like a Roman Catholic High Mass. The warmth, the unknown speech, the murmur of prayer, cast a rich drowsiness over me. The Bishop's gold shoes and crimson stockings, the embroidered crimson kerchief which hung from his wrist to the ground, his long auburn beard, the silk gauntlets, coloured like blood with the stigmata worked upon them in gold, the acolytes who held tall feather fans with tinkling ornaments upon them, all grew blurred in a dream. The elevation awoke me; the bell rang, cymbals clashed, acolytes shook their fans till the ornaments rattled like dice boxes, and the rustle of the *izars* as the women rose to kneel was like a wave breaking softly.

Then the Bishop, bending above the altar rail, gave with his two joined hands the touch of Peace to a member of the congregation, who passed it on to the next, and so on from worshipper to worshipper, row after row, through the whole length of the church.

Soon after that Mass was over. We crushed our way out into the narrow lane, and discovered that little Charles was lost. There was a hectic search, for the sense of danger is so inbred in the Eastern Christian that it enters in a surprising way into the least threatening moments of his life. But Charles was merely lost in his own meditations behind a pillar. He awoke to the ordinary facts of life when we stopped at the pastrycook's door to choose the Christmas cake.

Education

At this time I used to improve my Arabic by going to the Iraq
Government School for Girls, a place enclosed in high walls in
the quarter of the Haidar Khaneh mosque. I used to walk,
either along the narrow path that hangs above the river and
through the dark bazaars of the western bank, or across the
Tigris and along New Street, busy with its dingy morning
toilet and still comparatively empty. As I turned beyond the
blue domes of the mosque and entered the crooked lanes, I
would find myself walking with many little black high-heeled
figures, all hurrying the same way and unrecognizable until,
having passed the white-bearded guardian of the gate, their
lifted veils showed the smiling familiar faces of my school-
fellows.

There were about five hundred of them, mostly day scholars, with a few boarders—and of every age between five and
thirty-five. The majority Moslem, with a sprinkling of Christians and Jews.

The teachers, with the exception of the headmistress, who
has now left a very capable Syrian in her place, were all either
Syrian or Iraqi. Education in the Western sense is new in the
country, and the native teachers are still few in number: but
they increase year by year and begin to look with disfavour on
the contingent which, with neat Beyrout speech and French
clothes and city manners, comes across the desert from Syria at
the end of every vacation and brings a general feeling of civilization which their more Eastern sisters resent and imitate.

Among the various forms of pluck in this world, that of
these little Arab teachers deserves a mention.

They give themselves no airs of feminine emancipation, but at eighteen or twenty launch out alone into strange and distant cities: they find their own lodgings and make their own lives in countries where professional women are as yet unknown and quite unprovided for; and they do it with a cheerful enthusiasm which middle-aged people attribute to ignorance and youth.

If their teaching is not very profound who shall blame them?

It is, as a matter of fact, extremely superficial, and the more so because most of them are unaware of less self-satisfied standards. The praise which is so much their due is relative, but this they are apt not to take into account, nor is the distinction often enough made. That there are things in heaven and earth undreamed of in their philosophy never enters their mind. How should it? Their education, like most education in the Near East, comes from America. Humility is not its distinguishing feature. For its unimaginative shallowness, its pedigree, like that of Count von Bismarck, when he broke in on the Pope's councils uninvited, may be "an explanation but not an excuse."

I was put into the third class and in process of time was promoted to the fourth. Here my school-fellows' ages ranged from twelve to twenty-five: there were nearly thirty of us and we spent our morning hour over Arabic grammar and easy reading. To those unacquainted with the mysteries of Arabic I may say that reading is not so simple as it sounds: ordinary conversation leaves out all the terminations, and ordinary print leaves out all the short vowels: if you read aloud, you supply these deficiencies out of your knowledge of the syntax or else out of your inner consciousness, which is usually a failure. We used to spend three or four lessons over each page. The elder girls, whose minds were what is called formed before they had thought of acquiring learning, were frequently reduced to tears, while the little twelve-year-olds piped away triumphantly.

Education

Occasionally I stayed for a lesson in history, and was amused to see how the doings of the early Caliphs could be made to teach modern nationalism: an ingenious system of comparisons would point the moral, so that it was difficult to see where one ended and the other began. As a method I thought it had its points and made us far more lively and interested than we should otherwise have been.

Politics and language seemed to be an inborn passion in the children. A new word would thrill the whole class, from the teacher down to the youngest there. They loved it for its own sake; they would contemplate it with pleasure on the blackboard and remember it the day after: and I would think of the tribes of Islam many centuries ago, marching behind their rival poets, listening to the glittering alternate word-play as they rode, and shouting applause. It is a curious trait, this abstract love of language, independently of meaning or purpose: it has made Arabic immensely rich and magnificent, a great organ sounding in empty spaces for its own pleasure alone.

One day as I came to my classroom I found two-thirds of it in tears. Rows of children sobbed at their desks, their heads buried in their arms. A quavering voice in one corner trailed away unsteadily, but no one was paying any attention to the parsing of verbs.

"What on earth has happened?" I asked.

The teacher smiled apologetically.

"It is nothing," she said. "It is the quarterly exam. It is always like this. We have had the results this morning."

Rather appalled to see learning taken so seriously, I sat down beside the little black girl from Basra whose desk I shared, and offered my handkerchief sympathetically. She was in a moist condition, having come down rather badly, since her facts, though confident, were always palpably wrong. She wore grey cotton gloves, with a glass ring outside them, and she continued to weep into them and my handkerchief while the teacher and I and the few who had come unscathed out of the catastrophe carried on the lesson as best we could.

I came away into the sunlit court, and wondered about it all.

It was a peaceful scene. The children were playing basket ball at one end. On the high roofs around, storks had built their nests and stood noisily clapping their bills. In the kindergarten the smallest scholars were singing nursery rhymes. The girls strolled about without their veils and abbas. They might have been a crowd in any school anywhere. They were well on the way of uniformity. Is that what we are trying to achieve by painting the outside of things everywhere with the same brush? It seems so, at any rate. But what it will accomplish with those fiery little mysteries who sob their hearts out for a quarterly exam still remains to be seen.

Ramadhan

In the month of the Fast of Ramadhan, Baghdad must be seen by night.

It has drowsed through the day in its languid bazaars. The sunset gun gives the signal of release. Then it leaps suddenly to life.

Refreshments of every kind appear as by enchantment. The owner of the coffee house, ample and dignified, comes out and welcomes his friends, while his boys in their long striped gowns and sashes, their skull-caps at the back of their heads, rush in and out among the fast-filling benches and clink their little handleless Czecho-Slovakian cups against beaked coffee pots, or carry painted glasses of Persian tea. Like stars in the twilight, the soothing glow of the qalian appears here and there on the ground beside some meditative smoker. Sweet-meat sellers set out portable booths at street corners. The greengrocers stack oranges and bananas. And more than all others after the long day of abstinence, tobacconists do a roaring trade in little box-like shops.

The first part of the evening is given over to domestic privacy and food: after that it is the custom to visit till the small hours, when a late supper or early breakfast finishes the proceedings of the night.

British residents, dining in their houses or dancing at the club, see little of this nocturnal liveliness. At most, as they drive by, they watch the crowd in New Street made visible by more lights than usual and moving in solid phalanxes, among squeaks and hootings of the traffic.

But in the side streets, where only a lantern here and there

shows dim brick corners, and the carved lattices meet over-
head, it is just as it has ever been. Closed doors in blank walls
are ready during this month to open with the same uncanny
facility as once they did to Haroun and his Vizier. In dark
lanes, rustling with shadowy gowns and murmured conver-
sations, the Eye of Discrimination may no doubt yet discern
its Moon of Destiny, however enveloped for the time being in
a black abba and the darkness of night; and following, may
watch it disappear with handmaidens and companions, and
the fellow who carries the lantern, across a mysterious threshold in whose inky recess the negro slave yet holds guard.

Whether "the wealthy merchant's only son" still crosses the
doorstep with that peculiar and engaging rashness of his, and
what happens to him inside, I do not know: he probably
climbs upstairs to the first-floor room, where the master of the
house is holding an assembly of his own, and spends a pleasant but uneventful evening. It is no concern of ours. We, being
ladies out on our own, are respectfully ignored by the male
guardians of the door. We pass through its shadow; through
the outer court lit by a lantern on the ground, where the
master's falcons sleep, with hooded eyes, on their perches;
into the inner court of the harim.

The houses and handmaidens of Damascus still allow one
to continue the illusion of the old tales; but Baghdad has
become prosaic. The court, painted green and yellow with
white lines to imitate bricks, is not imposing or beautiful, and
the maids who stand in échelon up the stairs to show the way
are dressed with the most nondescript European drabness.

The long room has alternate chairs and sofas round its
three walls, as close together as they will go. It is upholstered
in the gaudier manner of the Tottenham Court Road. Little
abominations of occasional tables stand here and there with
velvet mats and photographs. Even the carpets are as bad as
can be. The ladies' dresses range from woolly jumper suits,
from the black native gowns, to the latest *décolleté* from

Cairo. For comfort one is driven to look at their faces, which
are really very nice, especially those of the older women,
mostly of Turkish origin, who still wear the two black ker-
chiefs tied close round the forehead, with points coming down
over the ears and half covering their hennaed plaits.

They all get up. "Peace be upon you. Welcome and ease."
We sit down, near to but not quite at the higher end of the
room. Beginning with those in the most honourable seats, we
bow separately to each, touching our foreheads and breasts.

Conversation languishes. The daughter of the house, very
modern with shingled hair and high heels, offers cigarettes
and sweetmeats. A few remarks, like pebbles dropped into the
empty space of carpet round which we sit, gradually warm up
into gossip. The older ladies really have charming faces, full of
serenity and intelligence: perhaps the serenity of quiet un-
crowded years of seclusion and the intelligence of people who
read less and notice more than we do. This range is narrow,
but nothing that passes within it goes unobserved. The young
women are not very good looking: Baghdad has none of the
Syrian loveliness, unless there is a Circassian grandmother or
so to explain it: as I sit, I wonder how the rather insipid faces
turn to that charming mellowness of age.

Meanwhile my neighbour points with her cigarette to a
rather grim dowager who is leaving the room. "My husband's
first wife," she tells me.

"Do you see much of her?" I ask.

"We meet in the houses of our friends. We are related."

"It must be hard for the first wife, in the beginning," I
venture.

The ladies near by smile indulgently. A careless husband,
they seem to think, is not so trying as a bad digestion, which
is what the next group is discussing. Both are dispensations of
providence, over which they have not much control. There is
some point, I reflect, in being able to shove one's husband into
the region of the Inevitable and the Uncontrollable; he ceases

to be a worry, just like one's unsatisfactory profile, or any-thing else that one has not had a hand in the making of and cannot alter. Perhaps that is why the older ladies look so peaceful. "Life is like that," one of them is saying philosoph-ically.

The talk of husbands has made the conversation decidedly more animated. We hear of so and so and so and so, their domestic triumphs and difficulties. The stories in this feminine gathering become so Rabelaisian that my Arabian Nights vo-cabulary, expurgated by the Jesuit Fathers, is quite inade-quate, and I lose all the best bits.

By the time tea and ices, oranges and cakes are brought, we are talking so hard that food seems an interruption.

"And so," says my neighbour with the charming smile, "when she saw that her husband would pay no attention to her, she used to put pepper every night into the baby's eyes, and its wailing filled the house so that it became a nuisance even in the new wife's lodging in the next court. At last it grew so impossible that the husband himself came to her apartment to see what was the matter; and when another baby was born in the course of time, she insisted on calling it 'Pepper.' But none of the men of the family know the reason to this day."

Someone now asks for music. The maid who sits on her heels in a corner of the room with a cigarette in a long holder in her mouth, and joins in the conversation now and then, gets up to fetch a lute. The girls of the house take it to the piano and sing alternate French and Arabic. More and more people come, till the sides of the room are lined completely, and we rise to go: it is eleven o'clock and we have more visits to pay. Our lantern-bearer wakens from his sleep on the flags of the court and steps before us into the shadows of the street.

Well after midnight I leave my friends at their turning and make my way home alone. It is always strange and like a dream to walk in starlight among the narrow ways: but now

Ramadhan

in Ramadhan it is fantastic. The whole city rustles and moves and whispers in its labyrinthine alleys like a beehive swarming in the dark. One cannot distinguish faces; the murmuring figures glide by like flowing water, paying scant attention to the anomaly of a European in their midst at this late hour. The extraordinary unity of Islam comes over me. These crowds are moving through all the cities of the East: from Morocco to Afghanistan, from Turkey to India and Java, they walk abroad through the nights of the Fast. In their shadows they are dim and unreal, less clear to the eye of the imagination than that Arabian Merchant who first set them in motion twelve centuries ago.

How firmly he pressed his finger into the clay of the world! So that these sheeplike figures still obey, moving hither and thither in the night; and make one think, marvelling at its range of mediocrity and splendour, of the power of the mind and will of man.

The Fellahin

In early spring, before the first buds show on the peach trees, a sort of luminous transparency envelops the distant city of Baghdad and its gardens. The pale minarets, the slowly swelling river, the desert itself with darker patches where fields of beetroot lie near the irrigation ditches, the russet lace-work of the willows so frail against the sky—all take on an ethereal quality, as of some faint angelic vision about to melt into its own heavenly atmosphere, some fugitive embrace of earth and sky which has left this print of loveliness behind it for the eyes of men. The blue domes melt into a heaven of their own colour; the palm trees, bleached and pale after the winter, let the sun lie quiet as moonlight on their spiky polished crowns; and everywhere there is the voice of doves, sleepy and gentle, reminiscent of Solomon, and soft as the grey feathers which slip between palm and palm, or settle in crooning clouds on every cupola.

Nothing is loud, nothing is garish, except young blades of the autumn-sown corn that push up with the violence necessary to youth if it is to survive in the competitive world. Among the mongeese, under the columnar stems of the palms in the late afternoon, they catch the light and shine brilliant as halos not yet cut out into circles—so much more vivid than any mere terrestrial object has the right to be.

Before it has attained to this glory, however, and while yet the harmony of soft tones is unbroken, the spring has come: and all the lands that seemed so dead and dun around the city are filled with the bent figures of peasants, squatting over the ditches, squatting over the beetroots and lettuces, squatting over the low brushwood screens that protect their plants from the north wind. Only to the digging do they stand erect, having facilitated it by the invention of two men with a rope to stand in front of the digger and pull at his spade when he wants it out of the ground, a method which is said to enable three men to do the work of one in double the time: otherwise they are anchored to the earth to which they belong, and seem unable to separate themselves from it even to the extent of standing up straight on their two feet; they squat on their hams with a small sickle in their hand even to the cutting of their hay.

They are reserved people, not enterprising in friendliness like the peasants of France or Italy, and too busy with their immemorial toil to turn to look at a stranger as he passes. Their women, dressed in black like the Beduin, with a small turquoise on one side of the nose and anklets to their feet, carry the produce to market on their heads; or, if there is much and it is far, they hang it on either side of a white donkey, of which the owner sits loosely on the tail. If you stop, however, and talk to them, they will wake from the dream of their labours, and answer in a pleasant enough manner, and give you news much like an English farm-hand on all points except the weather, which their piety does not allow them to prognosticate, even if the deluge plainly threatens; for they are still religious, having neither the self-reliant independence of the Beduin nor the weak open-mindedness of the town.

One day E. asked me to go down to Rustum, which is the Government farm near the Diala, to see the peasants celebrate their annual banquet with a bonfire.

We were still in the last days of Ramadhan, so there was no question of dinner till after sunset, and as we reached the whitewashed mosque of Rustum village we found the crowd already gathered in early twilight, and great preparations going on in the matter of cookery in the women's part of the village huts. The men were squatting about in ample cloaks, speaking little and quietly as is the Moslem way on a holiday, the only animated part of the scene being the right-hand corner by the mosque, where the small boys were all gathered in charge of the Mulla, whose preoccupied efforts as he moved among them with short-sighted spectacles and green turban seemed quite insufficient to repress their natural spirits.

The mosque is a little model mosque, rather like a dissenters' chapel to look at, with rush matting laid all over the floor, very clean and neat and bare: here the feast was to be spread, with no feeling of incongruity among sensible people who do not take their holidays as things to be ashamed of in the sight of the Lord, and probably feel that he enjoys the picnics as much as they do. Anyway, there was something of the old hieratic pomp as the great copper trays were borne in shoulder high, with mountains of rice steaming like Fujiyamas unextinct and large cauldrons close at hand from which gravies and gobbets of mutton poured lusciously. Then there was a great sitting down, a matter of some arrangement considering the number of the invited and the amplitude of the garments, which tend to spread like a billowing sea around anyone inside them who is trying to sit on the floor: but eventually every tray was surrounded by its circle of devotees and the serious business of enjoyment began, in befitting silence, and with a rapidity which makes one realize why half the Arabs die of indigestion. In the twinkling of an eye those trays were empty, replaced by oranges, and by a general feeling of relaxation and expansion.

Leaving the management of affairs to the members of his staff, who were joint hosts in the feast, E. and I came out into the court of the mosque: here the colony of small boys, at last subdued to a proper solemnity, tucked into things in their turn under the paternal eye of the Persian Mulla. Only the women, who are expected anyway to live on altruism in this world and content themselves with the sight of other people eating the works of their hands, had no official part; they hovered in the distance, watching as it were the steam of sacrifice, and no doubt wondering if their calculation of their husbands' appetites had left a margin over for their own suppers. E. felt sure it had, so that with a contented mind I was able to turn my attention to the preparing of the bonfire in the middle of the yard.

My education has been neglected in matters like arithmetic and correct behaviour of many kinds, but I was properly brought up to worship fire. I remember as a small child being taken out to our Dartmoor "cleaves" after supper to watch the "swaling," and to dance with my sister round the burning furze bushes as they flared into the night. And I remember my father, in camps among the boulders on damp summer days on the moors, building up his fire with loving art, making a little hut of dryish boughs, and sods of dank earth outside, and a hole at the top for a draught, and then the precious piece of dry kindling for the innermost heart of the contrivance, to make it burn. And even in the house, where he used to lay the logs from our woods on a bed of ashes and arrange a semicircle of peats behind them to radiate the heat—even there one of the earliest remarks I remember when he came into the room was: "Damn those servants! Why can't they leave the fire alone?" which is surely fire worship, of a kind.

And other fires, terrible fires during the war, when ammunition dumps burnt through the night, flaring at minute intervals and lighting the hills of Gorizia, and the cruel hog's back of the Carso covered with dead, and the far Carnic Alps, with a devilish unforgettable beauty: or flaming villages during the sad retreat, burning three days and nights under the rain along the eastern sky. Who, having seen such things, can watch without dread and awe even the household fire?

The bonfire at Rustum, however, was made with a happy carelessness by the mere setting of a poplar tree, or the top of it, in the middle of the yard, and the producing of several matches: and into the light, out of surrounding night, leaped the faces of all the peasants, with their eyes, brilliant and soft as the night itself, fixed upon the flame.

They were varied in type, because sometimes the Beduin when they are poor come and work upon the land, and their finer features and nobler walk still distinguish them among the rest: but mostly they were a nation of their own, with black eyebrows curved slightly like feathers, and faces more carefully modelled than the pudding-headed Sumerian of the town. "Will they dance for us?" I asked; and presently, after a little persuasion, the younger men lined up one behind the other and began to circle, chanting, round the flames.

The fire burned into the night, almost as high as the tree which gave it birth: it tossed sparks like a horse its mane, up into the unlimited darkness: and the peasants, chanting and jogging round, with a sideways jerk at every step, gradually forgot our chilling presence: one after another knives appeared, thick crooked blades held high above their heads: one of the effendis, a nice young man who evidently knew the secrets of the human mind, let off his pistol—which had an instant and delirious effect and turned the proceedings from a parade into a war dance.

The pace grew faster, the voices grew fierce, more branches were thrown to feed the flames, the short thick knives were silhouetted blackly, and more and more pistols went off, drawn evidently out of the civilized pockets of the young effendis and adding a frenzy with every explosion: if only it had been a real war dance with a village to loot at the end, looted it would have been—we were ready for anything. We began to understand the meaning of dancing, which fortunately one loses sight of in a ball-room.

This became more evident when, exhausted with War, two or three of the dancers began to fall into the softer steps of Love. A little boy in a yellow gown, with a red skull-cap on his head, was evidently an expert: with clasped hands he wrig-

gled his little body; his face sat motionless above it, old with
an expression of unholy innocence, as if evil were as familiar
as it was indifferent to him, since the very beginning of time:
an embodiment, he seemed, of this primeval art, handed down
on the Babylonian soil from the first ages of mankind, when
movement was easier than speech.

But presently one of the dancers snatched a black abba
from someone standing near by, and, turning himself into the
most repulsive female ever imagined, advanced to the duet,
while on the far side of the now smouldering fire the chorus
beat on two trays and a drum and prepared to join in with
interjections.

"Oh Ne'maka, there is no rose like you," sang the swain,
contorting his body with a crack of his finger joints as he
clasped his hands before him.

"I do not want you," says Ne'maka, leaping with unfemi-
nine agility to the other side of the fire.

"I am ground like flour before you," sings the swain.

"There is no rose like you," the chorus repeats, and goes on
repeating, beating on its drum.

"I will get you water from the river," sings the swain, now
becoming so very caressing that E. evidently ponders whether
it will not soon be time to take me away.

"I will make your bread," the swain is saying. "I will make
your bed."

But Ne'maka, probably right, refuses to believe him, and
with sudden leaps and crouching away from his attentions,
repeats: "I do not want you" at every opportunity.

"I will make your food," says the swain, standing quite still
and moving only his neck in the most remarkable manner.

"What is it you do want?" he sings at last, with the natural
exasperation of practical man in face of woman's nebulous
desires.

"Still I do not want you," says Ne'maka, and nothing could
be clearer than that: and a good thing too, says my host, for

heaven knows what the dance would have become had she relented.

The repulsive female now turned into someone called 'Aziza.

" 'Aziza comes swaying; dazzling in whiteness above them all," sings the swain.

"Like the ewe lamb of Halak, that runs after the shepherds."

She: "Him I saw by the river, beating his breast with stones."

He: "I will prepare you between my breasts a room that shines like gold."

She: "Alas, my mother's son, I am sorrowful; for your trouble is in vain."

He: "After the laughter, and the seizing of her waist, she became like an enemy."

She: "But one day he brandished his poplar pole, and all my branches grew limp."

He: "Oh, 'Aziza, a gazelle nurtured in my room and garden:

"Her locks are like creeping plants spread on the banks of a stream."

With the fire settling in its ashes and the drums still beating, E. and I left the feast, and found our way—out of how many thousand years?—to supper in the twentieth century.

The Nisibin Road

There is a very old caravan track which leads from Mosul by Nisibin to Aleppo. It goes back to times before metals were invented: it was a highway in the days of Assyria: and the convoys of silk travelled along it on their way from China to Byzantium when Justinian selected Artaxata, near Erzerum, Rakka on the Euphrates, and Nisibis, as the three market towns for interchange of wares between the Empires of Persia and of Rome.[1]

In the first centuries of Arabian rule this route still went through pleasant and fertile lands. The city of Mosul lay in a semicircle west of the river, with the mosque on a height at the top of a flight of steps from the water's edge. On the far side, some way off, was the palace of the Caliphs. Walls and towers encircled the town and enclosed a square fortress where markets were held. The bazaars were vaulted as they still are: the houses were built of soft white marbles such as Assyrians used to carve and such as may still be seen there in arched doorways. In the town was a hospital and many colleges: outside were suburbs and gardens, Christian convents whose sites have remained unaltered in the hills around, and the shrine of Nebi Yunus on the ruins of Nineveh itself.

And as the traveller left the Sinjar Gate, he would hardly think of himself as a venturer into the desert, for he would go northward through cherry and date orchards and plantations

---

[1] For the geography of these old trade routes I am especially indebted to Mr L'Estrange's *Lands of the Eastern Caliphate;* to Beazley's *Dawn of Modern Geography;* and Heyd, *Le Commerce du Levant.*

of sugar-cane, till he came to an old Persian city built of stone, where the roads to Sinjar and Nisibis divide. This was Balad, now Eskiu Mosul, on the way to Tell A'far. Here he would take the northern road and come to Ba'aynatha, the centre of twenty-five fertile districts, the richest and pleasantest of all Mesopotamia. And thence to Barqa'id with three gates and more than two hundred shops and many springs of water: and to Adhramah, in the district of Bein-an-Nahrein, surrounded by double walls and a ditch, with an arched bridge of stone across its stream: and so finally to Roman Nisibis amid fields of wheat and barley, famous for its white roses and forty thousand gardens, its houses, bridge, and hospital, and baths, its fruit and wine and. . . scorpions.

We will not follow the route as it goes on to Syria. It is known to many people who drive their cars into Iraq from the north, and Arab horse-dealers still travel along it in the slow old way, allowing a fortnight between Mosul and Aleppo.

But it no longer carries such a variety of merchandise as in the day when practically the whole trade of India and China had to pass through Baghdad or Cairo to be distributed over Europe. The discovery of the Cape of Good Hope even more than the Mongol invasions destroyed these caravan tracks, and one is apt to forget in the desolation of later centuries how populous and prosperous they once were. There was a time under Ethelred in England when German merchants paid their taxes in Indian pepper; and in the twelfth century boat-men on the Oxus accepted bills on Antioch. The life of commerce was a good varied life in those days, as anyone can see who reads his *Arabian Nights* with care: and those who prefer their history undisguised may remember how the poet Sa'di, some time in the thirteenth century, met a merchant at Keish on the Persian Gulf, travelling with a cargo of sulphur from Persia to China: there he was going to buy porcelain to take to Greece, whence he would travel to India with brocades, and then with steel to Aleppo: thence he would take glass to

Yemen, and from there would finally return with a cargo of striped stuffs to his own home.

The thirteenth century was late for the Nisibin—Aleppo road. It began to decline some time before, owing—according to the geographers—to the particular wickedness of the population of Barqa'id, but more probably to the gradual decrease of water in all this region. It is now mostly desert, and depends on rain and a few wells for what little it can grow in the way of crops. But in the spring it is one of the most beautiful countries imaginable.

You may ride there for days with the grass up to your pony's fetlocks and look down as it were on all the flowers of Eden. The desert space is yours, and also the beauty of the hills, for Jebel Judi carries a line of snow along the eastern horizon. And against the Tells which rest like green tombs over their buried towns, the daisies break in another white wave of foam, so thickly do they grow where the slopes catch the sun.

S. and I were invited by Shaikh Ajil of the Shammar, and left Mosul one fine morning towards the end of March. Our host in his new Chrysler, with his Nejdi bailiff Salih, his black chauffeur, and several rifles, led the way, and we followed in a derelict object driven by an Armenian. The Chrysler itself was no longer quite as new as it had been a month or two ago: its back wheel came off, or nearly so, every twenty minutes, and gave us that leisure to look round at the world's loveliness which motoring in the East so frequently provides.

There was an indescribable delight of freedom in this grassy land, swelling and sinking like English downs. The lines tracing out old camping places, the ruts of the Baghdad railway which the Germans had laid out, were marked in flowers. Tulips like little flames began to show in the grass, though it was still early for them. Anemones, iris, a blue amaryllida like a small lily, and a black arum with a peculiarly unpleasant smell which apparently attracts flies, grew everywhere. Now and then, the foreground shimmered blue like mist as we drove through a region of periwinkles; and nearer the ground a thousand tiny varied flowers filled every available space.

There is a ruin or two and the broken remains of a bridge at the place which once was Balad, and as one there turns north one still comes upon a few poor hovels near the ancient mounds, a continuous though sunken stream of life on these vanished sites.

Towards the end of the war a great misery walked this road. The Armenians were made to come down here, driven by the Turks to their White Death of hunger by the way. The many who died were never counted or known.

We are so firmly brought up in our childhood on the fallacy that it is the Good who get sat upon in this world that we spend the rest of our life trying to think kindly of the oppressed, and wondering why it is so often difficult. S. and I were full of sympathy for our driver as he pointed out the places where his people had suffered. But then he saw a chance, and while our host was having trouble with the incapable wheel, dashed on ahead. Even Abraham refused to take precedence in the lands of another king: how much more so we—mere women—with the chief of the Shammar in his own country? We made our man turn back and wait, and had a sulky Armenian for the rest of the journey. Shaikh Ajil, when he heard about it, remarked that it never was worth while to do good to such people, and voiced the experience of disillusioned philanthropists by saying that: "If you spit against the wind, it will blow back in your faces."

Most of the Shammar were away in the lands of Shargat: but the Shaikh's own guest tent and a few of his immediate following were at Tel Ijdan, a little west of the Nisibin track. The tribe's grazing grounds lie this side of the Tigris from Urfa in the North to somewhere on the line of Kut in the South, and the Shaikh declares that 70,000 tribesmen obey him. This is nothing to the glory of the Southern Shammar years ago, when their headquarters were at Hail and they ruled Arabia: but apart from political catastrophes in recent times, the centralizing of government and the settling of the Beduin on the land is gradually lessening the power of the tribal chieftains everywhere.

In the desert one forgets this. The old way holds because the old life is still lived. The fact that instead of horses two motor cars are tangled in the tent ropes makes no very great difference.

Our tent was a large double-roofed European affair, with purple cushions spread on carpets on the ground. Salih superintended our comfort, and we had a black slave besides, called Kanush. His face shone with a friendly fierce expression and he sat cross-legged with his rifle on his knees by the hour, telling S. stories about Jinns, of whom he had had personal experience. Towards evening, when the creatures become more powerful, we would have to stop, for no one in the camp would then dare to mention their name.

When dusk fell and it grew cold, a lantern was brought on the carpet beside us and we wrote our letters and diaries till Salih came to invite us to supper in the great tent. This loomed across the camp like a hangar in the starlight, a structure of black wool about eighty yards long with ropes stretched far out on every side to keep it steady: it holds 300 tribesmen at one time and is six camels' load to take from place to place. As we stepped under the heavy folds we came into an enormous space of shadows, with lights here and there among the brown draperies and white headdresses of the Shammar as they sat round lanterns on the ground. They all rose as we entered. Our host, in the place of honour at the far end, stood to receive us. He was extremely tall, and made even more so by his sheepskin "pushtin" and the long "abba" over it, and by the darkness behind him. There is something royal in the manners of the desert, and Shaikh Ajil, with his black beard and long black eyes, his great height and the wide folds of his garments, might step out any day from the palace of some Assyrian king. His uncle was with him, a gay old patriarch looking less like the conventional Shaikh than his nephew and more like Noah in a convivial mood. Beside them were three of an even older world—Devil Worshippers from Sinjar, dressed in white; they wore high turbans, and their locks carefully curled over each shoulder. Their chief, a young no-bleman travelling with five servants, was extraordinarily beau-tiful: his pointed chin and delicate features belonged to a diffent race; and the fact that these travellers were strangers among men who considered them unbelievers, gave an aloof-ness to their manner which made them seem remote in the everyday world, like travellers from some forgotten island of time.

We all sat down. Water was poured over our hands into a copper basin, and cushions were brought to support the el-bows of the weaker sex: two slaves appeared with a tablecloth of red and orange gazelle skins, and after it our dinner, on a tray the size of a smallish table, piled with rice and meat; little dishes of apricots, cornflower, gravies, and other odds and ends, were placed around. During our week's stay we never tired of this delicious food, though we had it every day, and though our host deplored the feeble female appetite as he filled our plates at one go with one enormous hand.

The business of eating is done quickly and in silence, and after that one washes again and rests, and drinks the Beduin coffee flavoured with cardamom—the best drink in the world: and while our dinner tray, moving at a remarkable rate down into the farther darkness of the tent, was being polished off by less and less important guests, till it ended with the household slaves, little Muhammad, our host's three-year-old son, would toddle up and seize his father's bandolier and pistol, and strut about looking absurdly small among the bearded tribesmen and the great shadows behind them. It was a charming sight to see the tall Shaikh gather his drowsy little son into his arm

[84]

and tuck him away into a fold of the brown abba, till he fell asleep and was carried out gently by his guardian slave, a thin-faced Beduin from the South.

We sat on, and chatted about the desert news. In the distance, red embers showed the coffee-maker crouching at his work with coffee pots like beaked black birds around him. The tribesmen talked to each other in quiet voices, or listened to our end of the conversation, joining with a remark here and there. There was the pleasant sense of ease which one still finds in feudal corners of Scotland or among some country noblesse in continental Europe: the ease which comes when there is no different *kind* of life to create a barrier and when other barriers, such as birth, etc., are so generally recognized that no one fears their being overstepped. We came to understand something of the difficulty and interest a great shaikh must find in his task, requiring infinite tact and judgment, besides much knowledge of tribal tradition and law. Ajil's son is a student at Beirut University, and his father told us how anxious he was for him to spend at least his summers in the tents, so as not to lose touch with his people, and to learn as much as possible of an art of government which rests entirely upon personal prestige. "But," said Ajil with a smile that was half a sigh, "when he comes back to us after three years, no doubt he will tell me that I am a savage, and will want to go and live in the towns."

The old order goes. Like the country squire in England, the Shaikh is becoming an anachronism: the Latin centralizing conception is ousting the old personal ideas which were common to our Teutonic forefathers and to the Beduin of the desert. It is inevitable, as little a matter for complaint as the sequence of the seasons, though one may have one's predilections. But I have often thought that, as far as Britain is concerned, the increase of our difficulties and misunderstandings of late years is largely due to this cause. For we were fundamentally in agreement with the old order: the differences between the feudalism of the East and that of our public schools and Universities was not so great as one might think: and there were many points of contact between a tribal chieftain and the sons of English country gentlemen who ran the Empire. The reign of the Effendi is almost as new to us in Britain as it is in the Orient, and it is small wonder that we now and then have hitches in our dealings with it abroad when we are not yet quite sure as to how we are adapting ourselves to it at home. It is certainly a revolution which has given the *urban* civilizations of the world a remarkable advantage.

It was the most delightful thing to wake up in our tent in the morning and see the sunlight lighting up the eastern half of the canvas.

S.'s servant brought hot water: it came from goodness knows where, so there was not much of it, but they put it into a handsome pot with a long and narrow spout which poured so slowly that one could think of it as being much more. The air was cold; we were quick in our dressing: there' was a mysterious wetness over everything, enough to make our unscientific minds conclude that the dew must come up from *under* the ground, and not from above as is generally supposed.

As soon as we got out into the sunshine the real joys of life began! There was honey for breakfast. It was put with our coffee and eggs on a tray on a stone at the door of our tent, and the sun on our backs got warmer and warmer as we ate.

Everything we could see around was young and fresh and enchanted with the fact of being alive. And there were not too many things to see round us, as there are in most landscapes: there was only the desert, green and new, on which our black colony of tents floated like a school of porpoises on a quiet sea. Baby donkeys, fluffy and mouse-coloured, gambolled about. Kids and lambs, separated from their parents, were sent off in nurseries by themselves with some diminutive shepherd in a striped abba to look after them. The Arab babies,

with blue beads wherever possible and nothing on in the way
of underclothing, rolled in and out of their tents; while, in
some unobtrusive corner where stones might not be thrown,
even the py-dogs had puppies, and added to the unwanted
population of the world.

"This is Spring," said the women. "This is the Arabs' paradise," and came laughing and chatting in a circle as we sat at
the door of our tent. This season makes up to them for the
cold of winter and heat of summer. For two months or three,
animals eat as much as they like all day long, and human
beings can sit in their flimsy lopsided houses in comfort and or
wander delightfully in the lengthening grass and its flowers.

We used to walk over the desert, usually with someone or
other from the tents to keep us company. We met Fiddha
here, a beautiful creature of fourteen or so, trailing the long
embroidered Beduin gown like the old songs, with silver anklets on her brown feet and a little pick in her hand with
which she was digging up thistle roots to cook.

As we strolled with her, S. found a piece of chipped obsid-
ian on the ground. We began to look, and soon discovered
that the low mound we happened to be walking over was
sprinkled with flints and pottery; there were shards on which
bits of pattern could be traced, in brown or red unglazed
colours, four or five thousand years old: they had lain undisturbed, covered over every spring with grass and flowers, and
the mystery to us was that they should be at the top instead of
at the bottom of their mound. There, anyway, we found them.

Shaikh Ajil now came up and asked if we should like to see
the well his men were digging. A shallow green hollow runs
along this landscape, with a series of Tells on the edge of
it—no doubt an old waterway under which water may still be
found at no great depth. The Shaikh was digging for it in three
places: if it were found, the deserts in that immediate neighbourhood would become settled land and the Beduin there
turn into farmers, as they have done among the Jehash close

by: so that it was a momentous undertaking which might alter men's ways. And this, indeed, is one of the charms of the desert, that removing as it does nearly all the accessories of life, we see the thin thread of necessities on which our human existence is suspended: things which we consider ordinary simply because they are indispensable, there appear with their true import made visible: food and fodder and the temperature of the seasons, so near to the terrible extremes of heat and cold which kill; or simple objects such as the two flat stones without which corn cannot be ground and bread made; or the vessels to hold milk or water without which drinking is impossible (as anyone may know who has ever stood thirsty by a cow ready to be milked with nothing to milk her into). What we see in the desert are a few permanent threads which, overlaid and hidden by many patterns, run unrecognized through our more complicated lives and hold them together: so that living there for a time, we feel that we are re-establishing the proportion of things in our own eyes, and rediscovering their values—and water especially we come to hold precious, seeing, as King David saw, that it is the lives of men.

The well had already got to a depth of twenty to thirty feet and a little group of tribesmen was standing on the grass while three men worked in its depths. It was a wide pit, about ten feet across, such as Joseph may have been thrown into, and three stakes met above it to act as a pulley for the rope which brought up baskets of earth: a man held the end of the rope and ran to a distance equal to the depth of the well, dragging it along with him and so bringing up the basket: he was naked to the waist, brown and finely made, and the whole scene looked as primitive as no doubt it was, since Abraham must have dug his well in exactly such a manner. Shaikh Ajil stood for a while, very like a squire watching improvements in his park, while the men came up and talked to him.

Then he left and, still in the car whose wheel was so tem-

peramental, went off with us and his gun to shoot bustards
among the periwinkles which, growing to the height of a foot
or so, swished like water against the running board and made
it seem as if land and sky and the hills of Jebel Judi were
washed by the same misty blue of spring.

The bustard is inadequately protected against its own stu-
pidity by a law which forbids people to shoot it from a car,
but no one of the tribesmen think of this. Shaikh Ajil drove
round and round in narrowing circles while the harassed bird
waited in the centre, like a foolish female on an island in the
traffic, panic-stricken while the road is clear, but nerved at last
to make an unreasonable dash when she can commit suicide
under three taxis at once: just so the bustard, watching our
noisy engine approach as it were, from every side in turn,
remained stationary, craning its neck, and at last rose slowly
to fly when the Shaikh's gun was upon him. We had him for
supper.

Nothing could be more peaceful than these hours of motoring in the desert, except for a qualm or two now and then,
when for some reason or another the landscape ceased to be
flat and put our black chauffeur off his stride. We stopped for
instance with half our two front wheels over the hollow edge
of the old canal bed before it became manifest that our engine,
though willing to go forward, was incapable of backing, and
a descent sideways had to be organized on short notice. The
car seemed to be treated like a camel and responded quite
well. We came back to enormous luncheons and spent the
afternoon idling in the little Arcadia of our camp, watching
our bread being baked in holes in the ground heated with
small faggots of thorn: visiting the Shaikh's two wives in their
separate homes with careful impartiality: playing with the
three little boys and with their cousin Cokas, whose name, we
discovered, was a compliment to Sir Percy Cox and will no
doubt cause trouble to Arabic philologists later on.

As the sun reddened on the horizon and lit the under side of the tent-ropes, and the green desert grew luminous before the coming of twilight, the flocks returned from pasture. They drew near from every side in the leisurely spring evening: the light caught like a halo in the round woolly outlines of the sheep: the goats, straightbacked and black in garb as churchwardens and with the same respectable stiffness in their gait, came in separate companies, while lambs and kids with frisking tails came in their own convoys and, seeing their mothers after the day's separation, bleated from far away.

Fires began to show as the evening deepened: there was a pleasant sense of security, the safety of the tribe lapping us round: beyond it, now formless in darkness, lay the homeless spaces, empty as the sea. The dogs kept guard on the outer rim, barking now and then, while women moved about their fires. And as the chill of the evening fell upon us, we also moved into our own lighted tent and waited till Salih should come to invite us to our supper with the tribe.

The Young Effendi and the Sentimental Traveller

"Surely, Salim Beg," said I, "you would not scrap all the old things just because they are old? Would you not select and keep a few of those you think good?"

"Perhaps," said Salim. "But I think that in a million old things there is not more than one good one. I think I would scrap them all and start again."

Salim Beg is a restless young effendi, neatly dressed, very full of opinions which have not given him much trouble to come by, and with manners whose off-handed curtness he has cultivated with care under the impression that this is the last thing in Western behaviour. He, and the thousands like him in every Eastern city, are perhaps the most interesting people one can meet to-day, since they represent the immediate future.

I first came upon him in the house of a friend where he showed his objection to foreigners by sitting in sulky silence when put beside me and turning his back as soon as he could. The British often turn their backs when they can, so that they should not resent retaliation now and then. In fact, if there must be such a feeling, the people who show it are preferable to those who don't, though one wishes that, in the days when we had it in our power to give them a model of behaviour, we had given them a nicer one to go by. However, I greeted Salim Beg in a polite manner when next I saw him, and found to my surprise that he came up, still with his imitation of Western curtness, but with an amiable intention. After this he was brought to see me one day, and it was while looking at the debris from various Babylonian mounds and at the odds and ends of antiques in my room that we started the discussion.

I have mentioned Salim because I happened to think of him, but the same words might have been said by nearly every young effendi in the country who takes an interest in affairs. They hate the old with an almost venemous hatred. It is not by enthusing over Babylon and Nineveh, or the picturesque untidiness of water carriers, porters, and Beduin, that one will find oneself in sympathy with the young intelligentsia. "All you look for in this country is what you find in the Bible," said one young man, who appeared to have been meeting more missionaries than he could assimilate.

I must say that I have a great deal of sympathy with this point of view. It would annoy us all if the people who stayed in our houses were so interested in our great-grandparents that the little efforts which fill our own lives with business and commotion become as nothing in their eyes. I know a quiet elderly couple who live in a house built and decorated by an Italian artist of the Renaissance; it is marked with asterisks in Baedeker and people come to look over it with complete disregard of the proprietors' lunch and dinner hours: in fact, it is so rigid in its beauty that the ordinary knick-knacks of life seem out of place there. It crushes its owners. They wander like inferior shadows among their ancestral ghosts and only develop a timid apologetic personality of their own when they descend into a sort of basement arranged with unaesthetic convenience, where, over a bourgeois tea, they forget the past and its splendours.

It seems justifiable that the young effendi should refuse so to be the mere showman of other people's glories. He has, on the one hand, the sentimental traveller who laments over the ancient East: on the other he has the Western official, the schoolmaster, the business man, and everyone actively concerned with present and future; these are as ruthless as he is, and far more efficient in destruction. Between the two it is natural that the young man should choose that which has in truth the greater vitality; schools and hospitals *are* more interesting than museums, just as living people are more interesting though often less ornamental than old masters. But granting this, it is difficult to see why the mere mention of the old should rouse such paroxysms of indignation.

Perhaps it was the fault of the sentimental traveller in the first place. He had his innings and took an unfair advantage of them. He travelled when picturesque antiquity still held the reins of Asia and, seeing the young ideas as they began their first feeble struggles here and there, uncritically and unkindly stamped upon them. And he had great power in those days when petroleum was less influential and books were more so: for it was he who wrote the books—or at any rate the more readable ones; and the imagination to which his appeal is made is of a more facile order than that which lies open to his opponent. It is a fact that people can visualize the charms of a tribal chief in native dress more easily than those of, say, a bank clerk in coat and tie and sidara. The bank clerk feels it, and being now decidedly on the winning side, would not mind unless he had got a terrible inferiority complex as well. For the sentimental traveller points to the old barbarian virtues with all their grim qualifications, and says that they are better than the feeble imitations, the things that, like Tomlinson's ghost, belong neither to Heaven nor to Hell, which now too frequently usurp the place of either vice or virtue in the East: and in his heart, if ever he looks into that antiquated object, the young effendi knows that it is true.

His inferiority complex is, however, a mistake. It is not by denying things as they are, but by putting them in their right places, that the young effendi might find a more secure and less arrogant confidence. He does not, as a rule, hit on the real flaw in the opposing argument: for the sentimentalist, when he brings the old and the new together, measures them unfairly by their momentary value, and not by the *achievement* of the past on the one hand, and the *possibilities* of the present and future on the other.

Minerva sprang fully equipped from the head of Jove; even at the time it was considered an unusual occurence. It is absurd to complain because the young effendi cannot provide such ready-made perfection. And yet this is what we are apt to do. We compare the finished Old with the New which has scarcely begun. If we expected the same sort of prodigy in French or mathematics, the young effendi would have no sense of inferiority in saying that he had not yet acquired the mastery of logarithms or grammar, as the case might be, and no one would feel that this disqualified him as a scholar or a mathematician of the future. But just because it is the vague matter of civilization, he misses his point: he feels bound to counter a premature demand for all the virtues by an equally unfounded assertion that all the virtues are there.

I think this is the reason which makes the young men pursue the old with such implacable hatred: and the pity of it lies not in the destruction of things which, anyway, are bound to disappear—but in the twist which it gives to their own mind. The attitude becomes negative instead of positive: they are more intent on annulling than on building. The European administrator, who also has no particular predilection for the antique, will wipe out a street because he has a better one to put in its place: the young effendi will wipe it out simply because it is old: and the two results are not at all the same.

One outcome of it all is a strange incongruity. While the devotee of antiquity goes about the country studying its people and its language, its history and all that has gone to the making of it, with enthusiastic sympathy quite out of touch with the living force that changes it from year to year: the practical man, who troubles with history in his spare time only, if then, and is busy with the actual problems of roads and schools and bridges—though he usually has very little respect for the young effendi and the negative attitude in general and wishes they would leave the proving of their civilization more to the evidence of Time and less to that of oratory—he it is who really touches them nearly in their aims and hopes.

It is he also who solves the problem, and, leaving old things alone when they are not in his way, pushes them aside when he needs something else in their place: and lives his life in the meantime.

But the young effendi does not live his life. He is taken up with the dream of the complete civilization and worried by the idea that, as far as he is concerned, its completeness is not perhaps so entire as he thinks he ought to make the world in general believe. He is rather a pathetic figure, an idealist in his way, as he walks down New Street to his office, his clothes so neat, his shoes so smartly polished, his manner, beneath its defensive exterior, so terribly sensitive to other men's opinions.

He is a pioneer, launching a mechanical universe made in Europe on this ancient Eastern sea: but he has none of the happiness which should help in the beginning of things. While denying, he has believed the foolish people who reproach him with his apprentice errors, not realizing that he has many years before him in which imperfection is still permissible, not thinking that to err here and there while learning is better than to be right in the immobility of age. Mistakes are small matters, to be taken in one's stride with one's eye on the goal beyond them; but he dwells on them with exaggerated sensitiveness and can find comfort only by shutting his eyes and saying to himself and others that they are not there. And that is why he is ready, without looking into their real feelings, to mistrust anyone who is in a position to find him out; and why, without waiting to see in whose favour the comparison might be, he is anxious to destroy anything that may bring a comparison against him.

But a good deal of the responsibility rests with the sentimental traveller in the first place.

The Devil-Worshippers

When the Prophet looked on Damascus, he is supposed to have turned aside from the beautiful oasis, saying that no one can enter Paradise twice; and yet if one coldly compares the two, the gardens of Damascus are not so lovely as an English countryside in spring. But one never does compare them coldly, because the desert gives to the one an enchanted value. And so it is with water in Iraq.

A clear little brook that you would scarcely notice in Devonshire is here as a rainless day in the Lake District, merely because most of the streams of Iraq consist less of water than of liquid earth, and you might as well be looking at rivers full of tea with milk in it. I like these slow yellow streams. As they silt up or shift in their lazy beds, they remove cities bodily from one district to another. They are as indolent and wayward, powerful, beneficent and unpitying as the Older Gods whom no doubt they represent: and there is no greater desolation in this land than to come upon their dry beds, long abandoned, but still marked step by step with sand-coloured ruins of the desert.

But to leave them, and to come suddenly in the northern hills upon some burn that leaps clean and white out of a granite cradle—this is joy indeed: and as good a one as any is the small stream which falls through woods down tiny waterfalls below the Devil-Worshippers' temple, north-east of Mosul, at Shaikh 'Adi.

Here towards the end of March the hillsides are covered with blossoming shrubs, a little pink flower like blackthorn and another larger one of the same colour, the size of plum

[97]

blossom, but growing at the end of spearlike plants like broom. These cover the two narrow sides of the valley as one climbs up from 'Ain Sifneh, which in itself is a bad enough excursion for a car: the track from Mosul reaches it across open cultivated country, intersected by deep gullies where water runs at times, and impossible to negotiate in mud.

When you get, however, to 'Ain Sifneh—which is one of the places where the ark is supposed to have rested—the road really becomes obviously intended for mules. It attacks a wall of grey ridges before it, threading its way up a very narrow valley where these pale shrubs, delicate as the dreams amid our everyday labour, blossom between the boulders on the slopes. Here the soil is rock; alluvial Iraq is below us; and the water runs grey as the tumbled steepness around it, but clear, with transparent pools.

All this is Yezidi country, and the first of their peculiar tombs, with the squat, white-fluted steeple, is on a ridge near 'Ain Sifneh. We have seen their men on the plain below, dressed voluminously in white, with red turbans on their heads, and loose locks that give a witchlike expression to the long face and pointed chin of the race.

They are a peaceful agricultural people used to persecution. The respect paid to the Devil in most countries is unofficial, and the Yezidis are mere unbelievers to the Moslem, not People of the Book, like Jew or Christian. Historically their records do not go back very far. Shaikh 'Adi himself is supposed to have lived some time in the twelfth century, and his predecessors are vague and half mythical. The local tradition has it that they are a remnant of the Ommayads, and that their worship of Satan originated in a dictum of their saint, who once said: "Curse no one, not even the devil." Their choice of a patron has given them peculiar and harmless superstitions, such as their dislike for blue, the divine colour, and their avoidance of lettuce and radishes, two plants which refused to hide Satan beneath their leaves when he fled from the Almighty. Actually they probably belong to some very old pre-Islamic and pre-Christian worship, and as we climb up by one fold after another into deeper and more rocky recesses of the valley and into greater solitude, we feel that we are visiting the original dwellers of the land in their last inaccessible home.

It is not at all inaccessible, as a matter of fact, but only looks so. The car goes to within twenty minutes of the tombs of Shaikh 'Adi itself; we see the white steeples through leafless woods of March well above us in the little mountain valley. There is something pleasantly northern in its bare look after the perpetual dusty green of palms in the plain below. The twigs are plum-coloured like March woods in England: the trees are varied—fig and oak and many other kinds growing all together: they keep to the neighbourhood of the water, covering it with shadow as it falls in brown pools full of dead autumn leaves. Brambles and bushes close it in below: and where the ground opens out towards grey boulders which stick over all this landscape as thick as pins in a pincushion, we see that it is all carpeted with yellow flowers, and anemones, and scillas.

It is as peaceful a little valley as you could find in the Maritime Alps, with the same stony nakedness around it. And it is strange to think that the tiny hamlet nestling there with its two steeples should be reverenced as far north as Russia and as far west as Aleppo, wherever Yezidis are found.

Probably the Yezidis were sun-worshippers at one time, and they still conduct a white bull in their spring festival round the white steeple of their saint. The Shaikh ash-Shams, the Sun-Shaikh, is among the names they mention in their prayers, together with those of Jesus and Mary and many Moslem holy ones—protective names in less tolerant times. They by no means deny the orthodox saints, nor the existence of a beneficent Omnipotence above them: but they hold that the Spirit of Evil has been given a free hand in the world for the time being—a theory which one must admit may be heard on the lips of quite respectable people of every persuasion at the present day without the necessity of a pilgrimage to Shaikh 'Adi. The Devil-Worshippers, however, introduce an Oriental touch into this blameless conservative attitude by maintaining the advisability of making up to whoever is in power: they do not stand out against the works of darkness, like the *Morning Post*, but have built a temple and do their best to conciliate what has so remarkable a capacity for unpleasantness: and they neglect the Divinity whose leniency is well known and who can be trusted to pardon. *"Il nous pardonnera,"* say they, like Heine on his death-bed, *"c'est son métier."*

Whatever their theories, the atmosphere of Shaikh 'Adi is one of peace. Its small stone hovels seem asleep under their trees, listening to the voice of the brook below and to innumerable birds. In the stone tanks where Yezidis are baptized the sacred newts, speckled and fat, lie with that meditative placidity which the secure feeling of holiness should give; and beyond, through a gateway, under a trellis of vines, are two little paved courts that precede the temple.

The door of the temple is a new marble affair: but the walls are old and incised with carved signs, and I have been told by Chaldean priests that it was once one of their churches. In that case the black snake carved in relief beside the doorpost was presumably added later. It is the same sort of snake one finds on bronze handles of ancient daggers in Luristan or on prehistoric earthenware from Nihavend: and the Yezidis here, whatever may have been their first origin, certainly now seem to have more affinity with Kurdistan on the east than with the Semitic south, and talk Kirmanji among themselves.

The Shaikh of the place was dressed in white with a turban a little wider and shallower than those worn by Moslems. He took us to the temple. His sister, also in white, with her mouth covered and her head swathed like a nun, waited under the vines outside with two tall Fakirs, who rank below a Shaikh and wear black. Above the Shaikh in the religious hierarchy is the Pir, and at the head of the Pirs and of the Yezidis in general is the Amir, who lives at Badri on the western side of the hills, and has a peacock, their sacred emblem, drawn in red ink on his visiting cards.

We saw as much of their temple as they wished to show us. The water, which is supposed to flow there from Zemzem in Mekka, is not visible to strangers, though it has as a matter of fact been seen by several travellers. But the interior of the Devil's temple is a gloomy place, with a floor of damp earth on which oil drips from square metal dishes suspended here and there, with a floating wick sticking out at one corner. By this dim light we saw in bare alcoves the tattered draperies of the tombs, and wondered, as often one does in this land, what fervour of imagination can clothe such naked relics with glamour: like a child with its doll of sticks and rags, they need no external help of beauty to dress their holy things.

It is always better to step over and not on to a threshold in the East, and our guide asked us particularly not to tread on this one: the weight of two rupees was not considered a desecration. As we performed the gymnastic carefully—for the threshold is high—and came out of the gloomy dullness of Satan's house, the peace of the little valley again fell upon us. The white sister and the two black Fakirs and several small Yezidis were waiting in a group by the well under the vines.

We sat there with them chatting in the sun, asking about the life of the sanctuary and explaining our own social status in return. My two friends both possess husbands in the Civil Service, which inspires respect: but I was unexpectedly exalted by the fact of not having a husband at all. When, after some doubt, this phenomenon was finally accepted as true, the three holy men and the white sister admired me with wonder as one who has obtained peace in this world and all sorts of advantages in the next. "You are a nun as I am," said the white lady, looking across to me with the kind and quiet eyes that come to old age in the hills. "It is well to have left the world so young."

I felt unworthy in every way, but what can one say on such occasions? As we rose to go they presented one of us with a rosary.

It was altogether monastic round the temple of Satan and very like some of those remote sanctuaries in the Italian hills which sleep peacefully through the year until the week or so of their pilgrimage comes round. So the priests of Shaikh 'Adi wait for their spring and autumn festivals, when the pilgrims come up over the passes and the ancient rites are held. Layard saw the valley at such a time, filled all night with moving lights among the trees, which must be a charming sight. As for us, we walked down in the mountain solitude of the spring afternoon, peopled only with the sound of the water and the voices of birds: we looked out across the bottom of the valley, to the hills of Bavian, mauve and blue, with cultivated patches below their rocks: and over it all lay the sunlight, shining impartially on all temples of mankind.

The Death of Mandali

I suppose that, after the passion of love, water rights have caused more trouble than anything else to the human species. Our word for rival, or rivalry, comes from the Latin *riva*—the bank or margin of a stream—and the justice of the derivation is proved at any rate in Iraq, where the growing of rice is forbidden this year in several districts because quarrels over irrigation ditches lead to too many problems.

Where there are no running streams, and wells are few and insufficient, as on the borders of Najd, there seems to be no solution except a series of small wars and fights whenever the weather is unusually dry. But the matter of rivers is comparatively simple: the man above takes what he likes, and the man below gets what he can, and the former has the best of the bargain, as we have long ago noticed in Egypt and Sudan.

Whoever wishes to study this etymology of *riva* in the making, and to see the innocent Latin word turning visibly from a river bank into an international complication, need only go east from Baghdad to Mandali or Bedrah on the Persian border, and watch their palm gardens turning yellow as the result of the misguided passion for straight lines of former frontier commissions. This is not the only cause: the acquisition of a garden and estate by the Shah, and the increase in agriculture on the far side of the boundary, have intensified the catastrophe; and long ago, even when Iraq held far greater stretches of the river course than now, there must have been difficulties, though in those elastic days they were dealt with by Turkish troops and the men of Mandali themselves, who marched up into Persia every spring and destroyed the enemy crops, so obviating the necessity for irrigation altogether and the consequent monopoly of the water supply on the wrong side of the frontier.

There is something that wrings the heart in the slow death of inanimate things that have cost so much time and trouble, so many human years. Mandali lies on the edge of the desert like a sea-town on the sea: the hills behind it, delicate sharp ranges, form a coastline powdered with snow in early spring; the yellow level spaces sweep in a wide bay up to the lip of its gardens, that spread in miles of fronds at the water's edge as it were. In among them, the narrow mud streets, the bazaar with rickety wooden outhouses for shade, the tiny synagogue and mosque, and all the business of life, are dwindling and dying year by year with the vanishing harvests.

The orange trees have been cut down within the last two years; the date palms, the best in Iraq, every one of which used to pay four annas in taxes, have now been reduced to one anna, since the fate of Mandali is recognized even in Parliament. Industry, except for the stitching of Persian shoes and the weaving of a few pink and yellow jajims, there is none; and the small amount of Persian trade—which used to wind down the river valley over the shallow pass of Jebel Hamrin, where two police posts look at each other across a windy space—the Persian trade has been killed three months ago by the involved contortions of Persian economics.

It is perhaps a provision of nature that one hardly ever sees what is happening under one's nose, or life would be insupportable: our pains and pleasures belong to the immediate past rather than to the present, and since we only realize them when they have become inevitable, we bear them more easily: like the later Roman Empire, the population of Mandali, though they know in a theoretical way that they are doomed to destruction or exile, still sit in the sun on the long wooden benches of their cafés and enjoy themselves.

But we who come freshly among them see clearly the inevitable doom stretched over their living gardens; and likewise see, in our mind, the myriad dead cities of the desert, once ensconced in just such a frame of trees: they also, by the slow decay of rivers, or careless tread of armies, the deviation or breaking down of banks, came to their end, and are now mere wrinkles so faint under the sand that only the passing airman sees them from above. The inexorable science of geography is suddenly borne in upon us; with what relentless blindness it crushes or expands the lives of men!

Forty-five years ago the last lion was shot in the lands of Balad Ruz. At that time a swamp stretched from there to Mandali; one was rowed across lagoons of water in a bellum. Then a regulator was put to the canal north of it: the water drained away of its own accord: the lions disappeared together with the reedy growths they liked: and the swampy land became divided into cultivation and desert.

Irrigation engineers wander about with their little set of instruments, casting their bread, as it were, upon the waters and scarcely seeing, even with the eye of faith, the greatness of the revolutions that may follow in their track. But I can imagine that there is no firmer pleasure than that of building aqueducts or digging waterways in a thirsty land; and perhaps in later years, as a Retired Official, to look upon ploughed stretches of young corn in the sun, created by our labour in the resurrected waste.

This sort of pure and useful pleasure is open to lots of people in Iraq, and might with profit be indulged in by many members of the Government in various degrees. But here, as elsewhere, agriculture and irrigation are as much taken for granted and as little enthused over as the domestic virtues: there is none of the commanding rapture which is their due, and which is exclusively monopolized by destructive things like armies.

Perhaps it is something wrong with our religion, both Christian and Moslem, which has forgotten the holiness of the seasons in their fruitfulness, and has ceased to honour with proper ceremonies the mysterious birth and growth of the things whereby we live: so that we have come to consider human values only, and have left it to the scientist and the peasant to look upon the world in perspective.

If this were not so, the Naqib of Mandali in his neat cashmere gown, with the crimson lining and the green Seyid's band round his head, would not be watching so sadly his diminishing revenues: his people, Kurd and Persian, Turk and Arab, would not be so listlessly unoccupied and resigned as they stand up to greet his passing down the tortuous streets: the vivid women's dresses, flashing like Hope under their black abbas: the brilliant gowns and skull-caps of the children who scamper in bunches as bright as new nosegays in the spring sunshine of the feast at the end of Ramadhan, would not have this poignant quality of something vital and fundamental about to die, and the Naqib's brother, who is a deputy in the Majliss, would not stand up amid a yawning audience when he talks of his lessening river and fainting gardens.

If Ceres were still divine in the eyes of men, as much fuss would be made over the matter as is now done when the Persians, in an impulsive mood, absent-mindedly plant some little mud fortress on the wrong side of the border; and the death of these trees, which produce as much positive good as any political economist and have the added virtue of keeping people alive, would be considered as worthy of international remonstrance as the massacre of at least six politicians.

The Kuwait Journey

People who live by a riverside have always two pleasures to command: they can look both upstream and down.

If their hearts are young, they can follow the curving bank as it climbs out of sight—up from the flat lands to greener downs, to foothills where sudden corners take the current, to where the waters are narrow in deep gorges, and finally to where, among gentians and Alpine grasses, or perhaps just welling out of shale at the foot of some moraine with *Ranunculus Glacialis* beside it, the first clear fountain springs whose gathered volume is rolling at their feet.

Or, if they are not mountaineers, they need only turn their chair in the opposite direction and shift the decanter a foot or two—for I assume these meditations to be carried on in creature comfort, and with something to stimulate the imagination close at hand—and they can let their thoughts drift down more quietly as the stream winds placidly past towns and bridges, by "beds of sand and matted rushy isles," by reaches that hold the sunset like a sea—until the sea itself in its peaceful immensity engulfs the river and their dreams.

Anyone with a contented mind and a balcony on the Tigris, or any other waterway for that matter, can enjoy these pleasures at will without paying for them. If they were charged for like gas at a penny the minute, no doubt the human race in general would enjoy them more. But we were not of those who ask for such commercial guidance in our tastes: and yet we felt that a time had come for more tangible sightseeing: we felt a spring hunger for holiday: a positive dislike for Social Duties: and so decided to look with bodily eyes upon the windings of the stream: and climbing one day into Imperial Airways, flew with our shadow like a moving bird below us, south over a maplike landscape.

There we saw the Tigris as it is, a snake of dull glass, with brown of every shade around it in mud and sand. Its coils, turning lazily upon themselves, as if they meant to eat their own length, lost all sense of motion from this altitude. We hung poised, as it were, over a boundless immobility in Time and Space: for whatever the history books may say, no one can look down on that inhospitable land and think of it as ever different from what it is now, the home of roving tribes.

There, a wide monotonous green distension, the Marshes lie, cut by black threads of water highways; with low rare villages, like small crustaceans, wherever the ground rises in a shallow curve above the waters; with boats small as beetles pushing through the green froth that shows the tall reed jungles from above. And beyond the marshes, again in the brown desert, are lakes, lonely and inconstant and sterile, moving yearly with the floods and rains.

In the distance lies Basra, in a three-mile belt of gardens, under palm trees soft and woolly as green velvet so far away. And we descend—or rather the Earth comes up to meet us, with a surprisingness only comparable to one who, after many years of patient trampling upon, suddenly answers back: we stand upon her with a new respect, glad to find her solid under foot; and next day again go south over her lean spaces, the Arabian horizon before us.

The frontier of Iraq, beside an oasis so small that the desert light washes through it like a sieve, is passed. We are in the little buffer state of Kuwait which is nothing but desert and sea. And in the evening, as we climb the low sulphur cliffs in our car, the Persian Gulf lies beyond white dunes of sand. It is green in the twilight, with a salty smell: it is genuine sea. It throws up a dust of glistening shells for sand, and at its edge are tufts of rushes. It lies in an immense and happy loneliness.

The Kuwait Journey

Our petrol has given out. But the walls of the town are there in the last of the daylight, and here in a lorry advancing are three Arabs with black and mahogany profiles, and red kefiehs on their heads, prompt in their courteous way to offer petrol in a mug, and cigarettes to the Master of the Harim, while their faces turn carefullly from those three Immodest Ones, whom he allows to travel unveiled.

On three sides the town of Kuwait is surrounded by walls and towers, with curtains, or whatever the military term may be, in front of each of the three gates. In the darkness, through which one feels nevertheless the transparent whiteness of sand, the Arabs on guard are waiting for us; they ask for the second car, which is behind, gathering petrol by the way-side—the one Christian precept which every Arab chauffeur invariably carries out being that of taking no thought for the morrow.

The walls of Kuwait are meant for business and enclose empty spaces where Beduins may camp in time of trouble. The streets are solitary and windowless, wider than the streets of Baghdad, with wooden gutters shooting out over them from the mud houses. The wooden doors have carved centre posts, and small posterns let into the panels, fastened with locks and bars. And the figures that move about are mostly clothed in white or black, with a touch of red for the head or sleeve: and a black African face as often as not, since slavery flourishes, if not so much from new importations as from old slave families who multiply, and provide half the pearl divers. In Kuwait one can buy a black baby for twenty rupees.

It is still a Puritan city. Its women are not allowed out of its walls without a written pass, in the interests of morality, and the other Element of Discord, the gramophone, is only just permitted. Smoking seems general: but the British Agent's drink has to enter under the uncontroversial title of lemonade.

There are no trees except a few groves round the Shaikh's palace at the far end of the town: and the gardens between the mud walls are so small that they seem inconspicuous as anchovy paste between slabs of bread in the less satisfactory kind of sandwich. But seen now in the night there is a sense of cleanness in the air, the meeting of the desert and the sea. And the fourth side of the town is the coast, with tidal basins in front, and rough breakwater walls, and the ocean beyond; and boats drawn up in a long line.

Who can describe the beauty of those boats with their high carved sterns? Or the feeling of Time turned backwards as one walks along what might be the Crusading fleet drawn up for overhauling on the sands of Athlit or Acre?

The long slender ship of the Admiral, the Batil, is there among them. Its bowsprit is rounded in a sort of disc; its rudder carved in the rough effigy of a horse's head, scarce recognizable after the many centuries through which the design has passed under boatmakers' hands. In a month's time, when it fires the signal gun, the Batil hoists the Kuwait flag, written in white on red, and leads the pearling fleet out of the basin down to Bahrain.

The Batil is elaborate and unique; but they are all lovely, built of shiny yellow wood from Malabar, with ribs often made of single forked branches of their trees. The Bum— which is a bigger boat that sails as far as Zanzibar, and is recognizable by its black-tipped bowsprit, has an ordinary rounded stern; but all the others have a square medieval erection carved with arabesques of flowers. A seat is often built at the back, and a wooden rail runs about a third of the way round. In the middle of the deck is a shallow altar where once a day rice is cooked: dates, and rice at sunset is all the diver's food to keep them thin and fit in their four months of labour. Fresh water is carried in great wooden cases, now on the ground beside their craft, with men hammering at them here and there. They will be loaded when the time comes, and filled with water from the Shatt. A slanting mast will be erected:

and when the oars are brought, lozenge-shaped, older than anything upon our northern seas, the fleet will be ready.

The different kind of craft is not distinguished by its size, but by the shape of the bowsprit: the bold and simple line of the Sambuq; the nick at the top which turns it into a Shu'ai; the straight-down keel of the Jalbut (our Jollyboat, possibly from the Portuguese Galiota); the Bagala, is stern windowed like the Taridas: little canoes called Mashu'a'a; and the Huwairiyah, the most ancient craft of all—which we did not see—a bundle of reeds, boatshaped, tied together, with a hollow place in the middle for the fisherman to sit in the oozing water.

They are drawn up in front of the sun-soaked houses in a crowd of lovely lines and curves: but they are homes of sorrow for all that. Half the divers are slaves; and the rest, once entangled through ignorance in this profession, never get clear again, but go on from season to season in the boat-owners' debt, for their food and other extortions, which are never paid for by their labour under the sea. And here and there you will find an Aryan slave snatched from the Persian coast, though we do not officially admit it: so that altogether there is a price on the beauty of the ships, and on the pearl's beauty, as it lies in its twist of red velvet in the bosom of the Kuwaiti merchant's gown.

The Bazaars are away from these sorrows, turned more towards the happier desert. The sun lies on them all day long, giving a quality of light even to their shadows under the matting of the roofs. In their centre is a maidan, where camels and tents camp, with booths for saddlery and all tent furnishings near by. And here in the shops are clothes—the dishdasha, with gold-embroidered sleeves, worn under the gown, or thaub, which is a beautiful garment with bars of contrasting colour let into it, and triangles of embroidery put somewhere down by one's knees, where the wide sleeve ends. The sleeve is twisted over the head like a veil, and makes the thaub fall in long lines which the women trail behind them as desert poets describe it in the days of the Ignorance, before Muhammad. They are mostly made of Chinese silk, or silk waste from Persia. There are Persian turquoises on jewels with bosses of gold, or worked like the right-angled daggers of Bahrain with the sort of filigree found in the graves of Ur. There are nose rings strung with small rough pearls with turquoise discs between them. Frankincense from Hadhramaut, and incense burners from Riadh, of a size easy to hand round to perfume the beards of the assembled company, and studded like the pommels of the camel saddles with a dust of small silver crumbs. There are copper and brass things, for which the metal comes from Persia; and big chests of the Gulf, with beaten brass patterns and studded nails—made with Indian woods. For all the wood and practically all the water is brought across the sea.

The Harim went quite mad among so many fascinations, and strolled about with coral and pearls in its hands amid a crowd that walked with it in a mass: while the Master of the Harim with a patience impossible sufficiently to extol, read Bernard Shaw's *Methusaleh* in the car. But at last it became absolutely necessary to leave the Kuwait bazaars, if one was going to camp near the borders of Najd that day.

Through quiet sun-eaten streets, by the gate where the wall and its regular towers stretch to the sea, over the shining sand, we drove southward.

Here and there were villages on the shore, with broken walls and small gardens of tomatoes and onions—Kuwait's only fruit—and tamarisks and a palm or two standing at ease and haphazard, as if in a park in the sand.

But mostly it was Solitude, the desert alone with gentle undulations, and Arfaj shrubs just breaking into buds of leaf and yellow flower. On our left the sea, blue as the Virgin's veil and misty at the edge: mother-of-pearl and white coral lay bleaching on its shore and spiky shells which once were used to make lamps for the Sumerians.

Water seemed to lie before us, but it was only mirage, the water of dust. We turned inland over a low rise, till the sea became a thin bar on our horizon, and came suddenly on the welcome of home in the open space—for there was the group of tents in the hollow, and Beduin women running out to meet us.

And here we spent two days.

It is difficult to explain the desert charm, so empty of tangible delights, if it be not the lonely delight of freedom.

> *Libertà ch'e si cara*
> *Come sa chi per lei vita rifiuta.*

You may say that any open space with not a house in view can give that same sense of happy privacy. But it is not true. There is a real significance, a glorious exultation, in the knowledge that behind the horizon, and behind it again, and again and again, for days and days and days, lies the Desert of Arabia. To stand upon the shores of the Atlantic and not know what lay beyond must have been a very different matter from anything open to us at present, when we realize that however far we go, all we shall ever find there is America. And think of yet earlier times, before the world was round, when the Ionian wanderer beside the Pillars of Hercules could look out over an Ocean whose boundaries were actually beyond the boundaries of Earth. Astronomy alone can give us these pleasures nowadays. I am prepared to admit that they are pleasures unsuited to a democratic age, demanding a rather larger amount of the world's surface than is now available for one person's amusement. When Najd is a network of charabancs and Kuwait is dotted with week-end bungalows, we will not complain. But let us not be told meanwhile that it is all one—that those empty leagues around us out of sight do not give a rare and exquisite edge to our sensations.

The day went here in delicious vacuum, fed by the thin and buoyant desert air and divided into two by the appearance about noon of one of the lambs in a state of apotheosis on top of a mound of rice and raisins and butter. This required some getting over: we reclined in meditation; or watched the little Beduin girls dance, tossing their long plaits alternately from side to side as the chorus sang verses in honour of the two Great Shaikhs who had come among them—the Master of the Harim, and our kindly host the Political Agent, in other words. Only when the sun fell westward did we walk out again towards the water wells, or seaward, looking for as-phodel and scented night stock or any other small plant that braved the year's unusual drought among the Arfaj bushes in the sand.

In the evening, when the camp-fire led us back, and the sheep and the goats and the camels, the kids and lambs, had all come in in separate convoys and slept or nibbled in the moonlight, the three men and the women of the tents would sit with us on the ground.

They gave us news of Najd. Kuwait belongs more to South than North. Even now its Shaikh was on his way to blaze a trail for cars across the Dahana to Riadh, a day and two nights journey. Najdi raiders occasionally cross the border, and some were reported within a few miles at that moment. And the three great local tribes, the 'Ateiba, 'Ajman, and Mutair, are all Najdi tribes. We learned their 'Izwa, or battle cries, and as we sat in the tent, the men spoke of the fate of their chiefs and the end of their armies, subdued by the great King of Arabia two years before.

On the ridge behind us, which was the Kuwait border, Faisal ad-Darwish, the chief of the Mutair, had camped at that time. He had almost made the King of Najd in his youth, and had become more powerful than is wise, and being defeated, and wounded on the battlefield, had been given leave to creep to his tribe to die. But he did not die, and lay recovering in secret, waiting his time: and when the moment seemed good, came with his herds and his women, and many thousand tents, here to the ridge, and asked that the territory of Kuwait, which he had often harried, might be open to give them food. The British closed Kuwait, and sealed the fate of Faisal, and the Mutair is now a broken tribe: Faisal himself has died at the court of his conqueror. But at the end of the struggle, when the desert was starving them, they came again to the Kuwait ridge, a gaunt crowd, to beg that the town might be opened: and our host, who knew them well, went to press the surrender and tell them that there could be no hope. In the great tent, while this news was being faced in silence, Faisal's wife gave an order; the favourite mare was led out, and shot to save her from captivity.

That was the end of the Mutair. The chiefs of the 'Ateiba and 'Ajman had been encompassed before. They had both retreated to their own deserts after the battle in which Faisal was wounded, and Ibn Saud had given out that the Mutair was scattered and its chief killed, as indeed he believed. He asked the other two to submit. Ibn Humeid of the 'Ateiba did so, and is a prisoner now.

But Dhaidan el-Hathlain, a wily man and chief of the 'Ajman, was not to be enticed. Fahd, the son of the Governor of Hasa, came to him with a small force of 700 men, and found him in his own country encamped among 5,000 of his own tribe, and there handed him a letter from his father Abdullah bin Jaluwi as-Saud, promising safety on the word of the King, whose letter also was enclosed, and asking him to return.

Dhaidan with only seven of his men sat in Fahd's tent, with the 'Ajman camped at some little distance all around them. He was drinking coffee and thought himself safe.

"When 'Abd al Aziz (Ibn Saud) was a boy," he said, "I taught him to catch rats and lizards in the sand. But I am not to be trapped in the same way." Whereupon in the midst of his own people, and in the guest tent, Fahd seized and shackled him.

Dhaidan said: "If I am not back at sunset in my tent, my people will know that I am killed. I told them so. You are only seven hundred. Not one of you will be left alive."

But Fahd would hear no arguments.

The 'Ajman waited for their chief till sunset, sitting in his tent. When he did not appear, they chose Hizam el-Hathlain to lead them. They decided to use the sword, and knives only, so as to make no noise. They crept up, and rushed the 700 in their midst, and reached Fahd's tent just as their chieftain's throat was cut: they were only in time to rescue one of the seven with him, who later told the story. Fahd was shot in the face by a boy of thirteen who crept out with a borrowed gun among the older warriors. Of the 700, none escaped. And in the tent afterwards they found a number of manacles ready for the chiefs of the 'Ajman, and both Ibn Jaluwi and Ibn Saud's letters of safety, stained with Dhaidan's blood.

These are still the politics of Arabia. Not more cruel than ours, one is inclined to think when contemplating modern history in Europe, but possibly more sudden. They form the evening talk in many black tents, pegged down under the whiteness of the moon in their great desert silence.

Wolves creep up in the night. They will lead the sheep out by the scruff of its neck from the very midst of the flock, hypnotizing it with fear into silence, and kill it far away—a terrible warning to all the indiscriminately docile in this world. Three had vanished from our host's little camp this year.

But in the morning all is peace, and all went out to pasture. The camels, looking as if they felt that their walk is a religious ceremony, went further afield; they are comparatively independent, needing to drink only once in four days: the sheep and goats stayed nearer. And when they had all gone, and melted invisibly into the desert face, the empty luminous peace again descended, lying round us in light and air and silence for the rest of the day.

Time ceased to be. As far as we were concerned, we were ready to forget it altogether. But somewhere people in offices continued to hold to the illusion of hours, in spite of Einstein and all the Philosophers: they, no doubt, were already ticking off our absence in terms of days: their deplorable habit is always interfering with the rational happiness of others: and it was owing to them that the Master of the Harim, instead of leading his three ladies as they had hoped across the path of the Najdi raiders, carried them back reluctantly to Civilization.

Kuwait. II 1937

Aeroplanes now land beside Kuwait. Their clean and shining aluminium so close to the city wall makes one feel that history is treated as newspaper headlines treat grammar—the connecting links are left out. On the flat ground where desert borage and small grasses push their way, Imperial Airways passengers stroll twice a week with stiff and alien walk, like the animated meteorites they are; the air-gauge bellies out above the wind-bitten mud of the gatehouse: a noise of tilted petrol tins clanks in the sun; but the camel riders from Najd scarce turn their heads now to look at Modernity before the shadow of the gate absorbs them, where policemen ask for the desert news, lounging on a bench inside made shiny with much sitting.

The wall as a matter of fact is not old. It was built in 1916, hastily in three months against Wahabi raiders; but it might be any age, slapped up with mud, with an inner raised walk and small steep staired towers at intervals, and three gates between sea and sea. And the police who sit in the three gatehouses might also be dated as you please, Rip Van Winkles from any time except your own. Clad in what to the female mind looks like a voluminous nightdress very much "off white," amid whose billows the cartridge bandolier must surely get entangled in moments of crisis, the three old men lounge on their seat or squat in a windowless den brewing coffee and keep their eye on who goes in or out and, in their toothless way, uphold the rule of law; waiting for the approaching end of their days with that dignity which is the keynote of Arabia, made of poverty and leisure, and a complete unconsciousness of dress as an asset to respectability, or of physical comfort as an essential to happiness. As I stroll by and say "Peace upon you," they invite me to share whatever their meal may be, and send messages to the P.A., immaculately groomed and half their age, who looks at the aeroplane, unconscious that the three old veterans are referring to him as their father.

In the springtime most of Kuwait picnics in the desert and parties of women trail their black gowns and hidden faces under the gateway. Small donkeys with enormous ears trot in with lime and out with water: smugglers move about the village of huts which has grown up since the customs law of neighbouring Iraq has made the risk worth while: and, sight most beautiful, held no doubt by our unconscious memories from the very earliest days of tribal man, in the late afternoon the flocks of goats return with their goatherds, pour like black velvet through the nail-studded door, across the empty open space within the sunlit wall and its towers behind them, until they reach the appointed place where their several owners— who pay three annas a month for this service—come to disentangle and take them to their homes.

This open space within the walls is also used by Kuwaiti boys with time on their hands to lure the common little blue-and-brown kite from the sky. A few decoys, tied to stones, sit demurely about in the dust trying, like unhappily married Victorians, to look as if they liked it. Here and there near by, traps are arranged—concave metal discs that close with a snap when the spring is released which centres on a white caterpillar tied by the waist (if a caterpillar's figure comprises such a thing) who wriggles slowly round and round like a semaphore, succulently obvious from above. The boys wait at a distance and get four or five prisoners in a day; and sell them to children, who like to walk about with a bird at the end of a string in their hand; nor has all the missionary effort of Kuwait, over a period of many years, succeeded in eradicating this simple pagan pleasure.

Another prison, of a less recognized sort, stands in this empty space—the square palace of the dead Shaikh of Muhammarah, isolated, with corner towers. It crumbles away slowly in the sun, while a young Persian widow lives inside it. The marriage was registered but not consummated at the time of the old man's death, and the girl widow lives here like the princess in a fairy tale, still young but so poor that she will scarce marry again, with a fat mother upstairs and a huge old doorkeeper below to guard the pillared court and empty rooms, "with mothed and dropping arras hung"—the fading fineries and crumbling ceilings carved and panelled, the bathrooms and underground chambers where winds are carried down in shafts for summer coolness, and the wide roof terrace that overlooks the sea.

The palace was built as a rich man's fancy and a monument of friendship, to enable the Shaikh of Muhammarah to spend some time with the Shaikh of Kuwait whom he loved; and here and there in the empty rooms some trace can still be seen of former bustle, an old barouche in the entrance, glass ornaments and painful coloured fancies, mattresses piled high for guests, and brass-bound coffers: over all which, through hingeless doors and broken window-panes, the fine dust grains from the desert or the shore settle according as the wind blows south or north, and with their tiny rustling in the empty sunlight, give to the place what little life it has, except for the corner where the young widow sits dressed in black with high-heeled shoes on a stiff chair, and feeds her guests with sherbet, pistachios and melon seeds, sweets and oranges, and Persian tea, her pretty little whimsical face smiling with a natural cheerfulness inexplicable to the European mind.

Poverty has settled on Kuwait more heavily since my last visit five years ago; both by sea, where the pearl trade continues to decline, and by land, where the blockade established by Saudi Arabia now hems the merchants in. The Coronation sent the price of pearls to twice its value before I left, and the

British, who look after Kuwait, write at intervals to Saudi Arabia, so that perhaps a more lifelike atmosphere may yet run through the shipyards and bazaars.

March, when I was there, is in any case a time of leisure; the dhows alone, that feed the town with water from the Shatt al Arab, carry on their business in the small dry-walled tidal harbours, unloading fat goatskins on to donkeys in the shallow water. But the biggest ships, the bagalas and many of the booms are away round Zanzibar, and preparations for the pearling season down the coast have scarcely yet begun. Two boats alone were being worked upon in the open space of sea-front where the owner's house can overlook his labours. There the building is carried on as a family matter, with a clean smell of exotic woods from Malabar and leisure for the carving of posts and rudders and the flowery garlands that run round the high sterns: and, climbing across the thwarts to where the owner sits, plump and prosperous in his abba and white turban among his workmen, you may talk to him of friends in Oman or Aden, or inland merchants from Najd or Qatif for that matter, and find that, for the Arabs as well as the British, the Arabian coasts and seas are one great confraternity of intercourse and gossip.

For it would be a mistake if, deceived by such industrial tumours as the port of London, or Marseilles, we were to think of Kuwait as unimportant. The fact that it lies at the apex of several lines of good grazing to the interior and—equally vital—that it has good grazing for camels in its own immediate vicinity, makes it the natural centre for any trade destined for North-East Arabia: and this geographical factor is so important that even the strictness of the Saudi blockade has not succeeded in deviating the trade to more southern stations where camel food is scarcer. Even now, though he must do it secretly, a Beduin will walk into Kuwait bazaar and, asking for credit, vanish into his deserts with nothing but his word to bind him, and his word, humanly speaking, will be kept at the appointed time; and apart from this he will come perhaps once in the year from far places in the interior, Hasa, Boraidha, or Riadh, and renew his friendships, and call on the Shaikh who, together with his other friends, will all give him a garment, or some money, or pieces of cloth, so that his visit across so many desert days may not be a loss to him, and he may take something back from the city to his wives in their black tents, wherever they may be. And this explains how, in Kuwait, apart from the usual bazaars of an Arab town, there are miles of tented booths that cater for the desert, and explains the people you see lounging there in the inner carpeted spaces, with their guns in a corner; tribesmen from across the southern borders, their long hair curled on their shoulders, their eyes, distant and sudden as the eyes of falcons and as unused to the obstacles of towns, rimmed heavily with black antimony against the desert sun; and their manners as spacious, dignified and unembarrassed as the steppes which breed them.

In Kuwait you are still at leisure to notice what a charming thing good manners are.

As you step into the ragged booths you will greet the owner with "Peace be upon you," and he and all who are within hearing will reply with no fanatic exclusion, but in full and friendly chorus to that most gracious of salutations, and will follow your departing steps with their "Fi aman Allah," the divine security. Their shops they treat as small reception-rooms where the visiting buyer is a guest—and sitting at coffee over their affairs will look with surprised but tolerant amusement at the rough Westerner who brushes by to examine saddle-bags or daggers, unconscious of the decent rules of behaviour: and would be perhaps more surprised than any if they could hear how the oil magnate down the coast expressed his pleasure when some of the Arabs there saluted his passing car: "It shows," he said, "that they are beginning to acquire some self-respect."

Self-respect indeed! Where poverty is borne with so much
dignity that its existence is scarce noticed: where manners are
so gentle that the slave and chieftain are spoken to with equal
courtesy—no snobbish Western shading of difference! Where
the whole of life is based on the tacit unquestioned assump-
tion that the immaterial alone is essential: the Oil Company
may teach the Arab many things, but self-respect is not one of
them.

In a few years' time oil will have come to Kuwait and a
jaunty imitation of the West may take the place of its desert
refinement. The shadow is there already, no bigger than a
man's hand—a modest brass plate on a house on the sea-front
with the name of the Anglo-American K.O.C., Kuwait Oil
Company. Small camps here and there are pitting the desert
with holes, inspired by geology. But the industrial age is not
coming here with a rush, as elsewhere: its few representatives
are pleasant people who—marooned away from their familiar
atmosphere—are learning to deal kindly with a scale of values
so different from their own. The women do not stroll about in
shorts and sleeveless among the veiled inhabitants; nor do
their men shout abuse at servants unused to the unmannerli-
ness of European speech. Time is everything—and luckily it
takes eight months or so to drill an oil hole; and the first
experiment has failed: by the time the next is made, the Company and Kuwait will have learnt to cherish each other's virtues: Civilization will come tempered, more like a Marriage
and less like a Rape; and the poor little town—that looks to
her untried bridegroom hopefully for all temporal blessings—
may yet, with gentle treatment, keep her peculiar charm.

At present oil, like the aeroplane, gives a certain piquancy
of contrast. One bumps for miles over scrub and sand and
comes to a drilling machine alone in the desert under its aerial
scaffolding. It brings to the surface the unviolated secrets of
earth, spitting them out in grit and sand: and has a splendour
about it of human courage, here where hitherto man's day has

ever been as grass, "the wind passeth over it and is gone; and the place therof shall know it no more."

The drilling machine too is an Idea, stronger than the elemental matter around it: it bites away serenely, regardless of landscape or climate, the cynosure of its human devotees: and as one looks at their ministering figures moving about it, actively adoring, feeding it with grease and water, one is reminded of that definition of the Englishman, which will do across the Atlantic just as well—"a self-made man who worships his creator."

But the pleasantest of all things one can do in Kuwait is to treat it as its inhabitants do—as a town to be got ouside of.

Everyone has tents, and P.A. had his pitched—after several sunset expeditions to decide—on a low rise between the bay and the sea; so that each open door showed a blueness of water, and even in the white-hot day a breeze came wandering through. The lighthouse was on the headland below—an ugly useful little black modernity: and beside it a few boats so old, they must have been the first of all craft that ever floated— older, one would say than even speech or cooking. They are called hurjia, and made of the long centre ribs of palm leaves tied together at bow and stern; with shorter palm fronds put across inside and a second bottom laid lengthwise like the first a foot or so above it: so that in the open trellis work the water moves deeper or shallower according to the weight inside but never much above the second floor: and a sail on a slanting wand completes the outfit. No paint, nails, or caulking are needed: the ancient craft, the colour of dead seaweed, lie about on a tidal rim of small pink shells and watch the weekly steamers pass: they belong to the guardian of the lighthouse, a friend of the P.A. and old Wahabi Beduin from Najd, who would stroll up to sit awhile in our tent and offer dates and sour milk laban, and talk of what was gossiped in Arabia and of "the days of the Ignorance, the days before Religion," referring to the modern Puritan revival of the Wahabi Ihwan in words used 1300 years ago for the coming of Islam.

In the distance, Kuwait and its bay looked definite and small, like some early water-colour landscape. The heat was clean and strong, made of pure air and salt water: it lay on the tent heavy as a royal cloak and gave a luminous quality to the shadows inside. The servants came at intervals barefooted, in long gowns, with clinking cups of coffee. And in the sunset we would drive home. The town shone before us; its gatehouse caught the light; its walled security made the desert seem more open around it, with vivid green patches of corn that, for want of rain, seldom ripen, near the wells of the town; and every day afresh it seemed incredible that something so perfect and so remote still tangibly exists in this world.

In the sandy dust of unpaved streets the black-gowned Beduin girls sit, enjoying their leisure; the whitewashed houses as the light fades take on pastel tints rich and strange; the sea lies in pans of cold and lovely light in its small harbours, rimmed with black walls like the Beduin's eyes with kohl: and beyond them the line of the outer sea is already dark with night.[1]

[1] Thanks for information afforded are due to Lieut. Col. A. Dickson and Captain G. de Gaury, M.C., my kind hosts in Kuwait.

Failichah

At the head of the Persian Gulf, opposite the Bay of Kuwait, is an island called Failichah or Failikah.

How did it come to have a name so non-Arabian and so happy?[1] Even in its syllables there is a sound of peace, left by sea-wanderers who rested here long enough for the print of their foreign tongue to remain when they were forgotten. And the island itself carries in its atmosphere the same remote elusive felicity, a feeling of Echo, of something that has vanished not by violence but imperceptibly, so that an intangible essence still hangs upon the air.

If sound is indeed perpetual the headwaters of the Persian Gulf must be filled dimly with the noise of Alexander and his armies. Nearchus the admiral coasted up the map from Carmania, but did not reach Failichah. From the head of the Gulf westward his farthest point was the city of Teredon[2] at the

---

[1] There is an Arabic root فلق which means the opening of the pearl oyster: but I have never heard the ق change to K or ch. A Portuguese derivation from felucca is also suggested.

[2] The site of Teredon (or Diridotis) in 325 B.C. was, according to Nearchus, at a point where the coast, after turning to the west, met the outlet of the Euphrates (Strabo, 16, 3.2.). This cannot have been much south of modern Zubair. The port of Ubulla, which was probably on what is now the Ashar canal in Basra, is mentioned about A.D. 60 in the Periplus of the Erythraean Sea under the name of Apologos: Nearchus does not mention it, so that it was probably founded at some time during the three preceding centuries, between Nearchus and the Periplus, while Teredon and the old Euphrates estuary were declining together. Pliny (VI. 32) about the time of the

mouth of the Euphrates, then a separate river with an estuary of its own not far from modern Zubair. But after Nearchus, Androsthenes the Thasian travelled down the western shore and says "that on the coasting voyage, with the continent on the right, one sees next after Teredon the island Icarus, and in it a temple sacred to Apollo and an oracle of Artemis."[1]

Eratosthenes wrote this, and Strabo copied it, but Pliny later confused the issue with improbable mileage, so that the island of Icarus has been placed far down to the south. Pliny's distances are so misleading for other neighbouring places, and he speaks so palpably vaguely from hearsay that one is justified in preferring the older testimony, and in looking somewhere on Failichah for the Greek forgotten temples by the sea.

One should go there in March in a year when rain has fallen so that, in their shallow hollows, the sparse cornfields are green. The seed has come from Persia, for the blue Persian lily springs up in it, and sheaves of the red gladiolus. On open

---

Periplus, already speaks of "the *old* mouth of Euphrates which *formerly* existed." Being so close together, Teredon would scarcely be very important *simultaneously* with Apologos.

It must be borne in mind that the silt of the three great rivers, Euphrates, Tigris, Karun, has caused a very rapid increase of land at the head of the Persian Gulf. Pliny, quoting Juba, makes an increase of seventy miles in four or five decades south of Charax Spasini, now probably Khurramshah: this is a fantastic report and invalidates all his statements of distances in these regions (his unreliability is increased by the fact that he omits all mention of Apologos which we know existed at that time): but the fact remains that most of the modern shore is very recent, and that, as late as the tenth century A.D., the open sea came north as far as Abadan (Muqaddisi, etc). The coast ran certainly north of this point in the time of Nearchus; and he must, therefore, be taken to describe Teredon and the Euphrates mouth as *west of some point north of Abadan*; so bringing us somewhere to the vicinity of Zubair.

[1] Strabo, 16. 3.2. Pliny, VI, 32.

sandy bents small iris grow, straight between their curved leaves like heraldic fleur-de-luce. Prickly borage and pale convolvulus flowers creep over the poorest soil, where shells and mother-of-pearl lie stranded in recent visits of the sea. The island, low and sandy, is born like Aphrodite of the waters and runs to shallow headlands half submerged: the people's fish-traps, screens of reeds built into heart-shaped enclosures with an opening landwards, stand far out and show the little depth of these scarce shelving shores. Fishing boats pass by in open water, and the curved line that holds their sail, delicate and tapering as the stroke of a Chinese pen, slant across the straightness of the horizon. Except for one or two sidr or nebk trees, one or two palms enclosed in crumbling walls of gardens, nothing here is precipitous or abrupt: the lines are horizontal or gently undulating like the sea around them, and the small town on the western side lies with its one-storied flat-roofed houses, the sun-whitened mud of their walls and its prodigal spaces, almost as flat as the rest of the island and as open to the steps of the sun. Here, with the darkness of Europe behind one, a temporary peace may yet be enjoyed; for there are neither motor cars, gramophones nor newspapers; the land is free to any who wish to build upon it; and the fishermen, spinning their cotton yarn or knotting nets in the shadow of their boats will call "Peace" upon the stranger who saunters on the sand between the houses and the sea.

The best house belongs to Yusuf al-Mutawwaa', who comes here with his children and grandchildren for the good months of the spring.

One of the gentlest of old men, he lives on a respectable income made years ago by the selling of slaves from Mekka, to which he now—out of regard for modern convention—refers to as trade in dates. Six times, he said, he had been to Mekka, combining the investments of this world with an insurance for the next—and offered to relinquish the (spiritual) benefit of one pilgrimage in my favour.

Failichah

D.G., amused, moved over to ask for a similar gift, and was very properly refused. We were crossing to Failichah from Kuwait in a launch—a two hours' run. The old man, gowned in wine-coloured brocade, sat like a Titian Doge against a background of sea in which porpoises were playing. He wore dark glasses and a red kaffiah with black fillet on his head. His aquiline profile, grey-bearded, was courteously bent towards D.G. and another friend beside him, a Kuwaiti skipper with trim grey beard and thin and gentle face. The two old men, talking earnestly, clicked their amber rosaries in absent-minded, long-fingered delicate hands—the sort of hand, so fine and nervous, that makes it absurd to speak of the true-bred Arab as one of the uncivilized races of the world. From the front of the launch, over bales of luggage, one of the sailors climbed at intervals and poured bitter coffee into the handleless new-fashioned cups from Bahrain, which have an Arabic name in gold stamped just within the rim. The rest of the crew sat grouped under the Union Jack, flown for D.G.; at the other end, the red Kuwaiti flag flew out above the cross-legged steersman, in tattered gown—an Arab of the Gulf dark-skinned with slave blood. His cheek-bones caught the sun duskily under the red flag and hard blue sky; his scanty black moustache shone as if it were polished with blacking: against our luminous views of waters he seemed unnaturally vivid, like some rich venetian landscape red and blue—or perhaps it was just the holiday feeling of the day. For the feeling persisted when we were carried to land and sat at lunch in D.G.'s tent round hills of rice and saffron on the floor—and slept through the afternoon in Yusuf's house, that looks through blue-green shuttered windows eaten by salt and sun on to a quiet court with grassy patches—and strolled towards sunset to the shrine of Elias, a headland on the sea.

Elias, or Khidhr, is one of the most elusive and popular of Eastern saints—elusive because he shares with Enoch the privilege of never having died so that his body is non-existent and his abode uncertain, and he is inconveniently independent of a tomb. Shrines, however, are built which he sometimes visits, and he is good for fishermen and childless women. His festival on Failichah is in the springtime "when the old year turns to the new," and it used to be a goal for pilgrims, especially from Persia and Baluchistan, till the temporal difficulties of Iranian travel came to interfere with such spiritual jaunts. But women still come and, when their child is born, send candles to burn in the three naked little niches of the shrine, and flowers to be hung there and a sheep for sacrifice, and possibly a lock of the child's hair, which is often used as a symbol of redemption in the East. A peasant woman from a village near Basra told me that, when it is a year or two old, they cut off as many of their baby's locks as they can afford and give their weight in gold or corn to the poor—the hair itself being put into a pillow on which the infant sleeps. These things come down from some remote antiquity, and the fact of the spring festival and the pilgrims from so far might, we thought, connect Khidhr Elias with the temple of Apollo: for the little square room and egg-shaped dome above it have crumbled to their original mud and been rebuilt many times, and their origin is forgotten: and the Sunnis of Failichah, half deprecating the idolatrous flavour of the worship, half anxious not to offend some unknown sanctity, have marked the way to the shrine with small heaps of seaweed along the open shore—an offering touching in its poverty—and rebuilt the shrine itself with money sent by grateful mothers, so that their minute temple stands in ever-renewed loneliness and newness, like a small human query uplifted against the flatness of the landscapes and the sea.

There are a few Moslem gravestones near by, and potsherds, some of which go back to the thirteenth century or earlier, and farther inland, the ruined debris of Sa'ida under grassy heavings of the ground. The island traditions tell of seven vanished cities with a final exodous owing to a plague of rats, and three saints besides Elias—Sa'd, Sa'id and their sister Sa'ida. But Islamic history makes no mention of these worthies; the two old Yusufs shook their heads over them; and D.G., who is responsible for the theory of Failichah, pointed out the pre-Islamic Phoenician sound of their three names. We decided to make a grand tour of the island on donkeys next day—it is only seven miles by three—and to look for potsherds by the way.

There is a delightful feeling of security about islands on a holiday, like being tucked up in bed; though it would be horrid to be a prisoner on one for long, security being blissful only in small doses. Our longing to make it permanent is only one more proof of how little we understand our own happiness, ever accumulating the things which do not help us to live, ever piling butresses to keep life *out* from our starved anemic souls—so that the man who feels himself completely secure in this life probably scarcely notices the change when his relatives enclose him in the final stability of a coffin. This is the attitude I find so depressing in Roman poets who thought it impious to sail across the waters (and it was only their potty little Mediterranean they had in mind at that). But it is another matter to sit for a day or a week or a month between the coasts of Asia, shut out from them and their dreams by the arms of the sea.

We did not sit, but tried to do so, jogging about on seven small donkeys with that irresponsible feeling of happiness which comes in a roadless land. Perhaps it is some far Paleolithic or Eolithic memory, that makes the world so much more attractive when one's way across it is not marked by paths. We meandered over the buried sites of Sa'd and Sa'id and found negative evidence there—round pottery that might be as early as you please, and none of the later glazed mediæval sherds. Here we were told of beads and bracelets found sometimes when the ground is ploughed, and of an inscription discovered years ago and carried off by the Royal Navy; and

came to the conclusion that, of all the vanished cities of Failichah, Sa'd and Sa'id is the one to look at for the temples of
Artemis and Apollo.

But the day was far too lovely for these dim antiquities; the
corn too green, the larks too shrill, the desert and the sown
too full of flowers. The corn lay in patches unenclosed where
the soil allowed, so sparsely growing that our small donkey
hooves did little damage as they crossed the narrower places.
Women were out working, black objects in the sun. We too,
the ladies of our company, were partly and very decently
black, for D.G.—after looking dubiously on our efforts at
breakfast to sit cross-legged on the floor in ordinary skirts—
borrowed two of the most dilapidated black abbas in existence from the Yusuf household and watched with amusement
while his retainers, with obvious approval, draped us from
waist to ankle on our steeds.

About two thirds of the way down the west coast of the
island one comes to a place of low mounds called Qusur, the
ruins of some Persian or Portuguese fort with plans of walls
still traceable. Here—leaving Sabhiya, where similar remnants
are reported, on the south—we crossed to the other coast and
came to a little hollow of fresh grass with ducks and cows
about it, and two mud-built rooms on whose roof, beside the
Kuwaiti flag, a white wind-wheel was turning at great speed,
charging the battery of Shaikh Fahd's wireless.

This is the only modern engine on the island. It travels
about with its master—a cousin of the Shaikh of Kuwait and
an excellent English scholar—who sits in his tent in the desert
with his hawks tethered behind him on their stands, listening
to the news of the world. He fed us with Arabian hospitality,
on roasted lamb and pomfret—a fish they call Zobaida and
eat roasted or stewed deliciously with limes. Together with
carrots it forms the chief export of Failichah.

In the late afternoon the donkeys were collected, such of
them as had not escaped already to their homes. We jogged

Failichah

back with the little shrine of Khidhr Elias away on our right. The evening lit the ears of wild grasses, they bent in the slight sea wind and shone like metal: the light fell on the rainpools that lie before the town, where women dip earthenware round-bottomed pitchers of Oman, carried slanting on a cushion on their head. As we loitered in, an old man came out of a gate in the mud wall and asked us to his garden; secluded from the winds, a few nebk trees grew there, and melon plants in small sunken pits: rain had lately fallen and made all green. "The Spring is pleasant in Failichah," we said. "And your coming is pleasant—you are the Spring," he replied. As we came to Yusuf's house, we saw him in his gold-brocaded gown sitting on one of his six chairs on the open foreshore, chatting to his servants: and as the sunset faded, we went in with him to talk the day over round his coffee hearth on the floor.

The "Slaves'" Club

The negroes of Kuwait have a club where they dance once a week, on Thursdays. It is a religious sort of a dance, and visitors—who are welcomed in a friendly manner—are expected to take their shoes off as they step into the small mud-walled courtyard where the proceedings take place. A red flag with white star and crescent flutters above a mud hut at the other end; a small porch is arranged opposite, with a bit of carpet, and cushions made of striped ticking where the visitors are accomodated while the dancers' coats and cloaks are stacked behind: the women, veiled Moslem-fashion in black abbas, crouch along one wall, and the men, drifting about in the centre, gradually form themselves into a circle and follow each other round and round like autumn leaves in a pool, till the thud of their feet resolves itself into the rhythmic beat of music.

They are Nubians, they tell me, whose grandfathers or great-grandfathers have been carried across Arabia. They stand about, looking childlike and gay, dressed in nondescript European oddments over dingy cotton gowns. New slaves are no longer brought to Kuwait, and more already there to-day are free. The Shaikh himself has a body of these black servants, and the toothless, friendly old negro who runs the club was the favourite of the great Mubarak, a power to be reckoned with in his small court. He stands by the door now, receiving those who come, while the "band" prepares itself.

This is the *tanbura*, a venerated object like a shallow drum, two feet or so across, with two holes for resonance: from the bottom edge, six strings run across it to a wooden frame above, which gives it somewhat the look of a harp: little triangular things like pin-cushions, of many colours, hang in streamers all about it, evidently sacred, for when, in the ardour of the dance, one or other of the men feel that they are becoming "possessed," they stretch out their hand and touch the little cushions, and stroke their head with the same hand, and obviously feel better; or drag themselves prostrate and waggle their heads under the swaying streamers.

The *tanbura* has a thin stringlike note, and the bass is given beside it by a huge old grey-haired negro with a squashed tarbush on his head. He wears a girdle round his hips made of innumerable small shrivelled hooves of sheep or goats, with a few empty reels of cotton among them, all tied at the end of threads of coir yarn a foot or less in length: when he shakes his hips, they rattle; he holds a camel stick in his hands and turns from side to side making a constant swishing noise, while the drops of perspiration roll down his black cheeks into his grey beard.

The men dance now, settling gradually into a steady circle, and singing with sweet and plaintive voices very different from the harsh notes of Arabia. I wonder where I have heard that singing before—and then remember: it is the voice of the negro spirituals, lifted now in a language they themselves no longer understand, to their ancestral, almost forgotten gods. They sing and dance together, stooping slightly forward, jerking knees and forearms simultaneously, beating the earth with their feet in perfect time, so that the thud of it shakes the court and all its walls. One or other now leaves the circle and leaps about inside, wildly: the men growl, the crouching women trill their tongs in a shrill chorus: one and then another gets up and joins the dance, the sleeves of her black abba spreading out triangular from the top of her head, so that in the rather crowded circle she takes up twice as much room as a man, as every good woman should. In the growing intensity of emotion, the man who leaped about has succumbed: he falls like one dead, is dragged by the feet to one side, and no one pays any attention: when the *tanbura* stops and the men sit down, someone goes up to him, puts his feet together, his arms over his chest, massages him from shoulder to thigh with one strong movement and slaps him hard: and eventually he wakes up and leans against the wall in a dazed sort of way.

They rest now, and another man takes the girdle of hooves and the camel stick, which he kisses, and then stands up to perform. A few drums help him, but the big drum which the negroes loved to beat about the streets on their way has been suppressed. I am surprised to see a few Persians among the dancers, poor people possessed by Jinn or by disease, whom the *tanbura* has cured: they have to pay heavily, and then come and dance out their gratitude in this unorthodox manner. Haila, my maid, who goes to these gatherings, tells me that the *tanbura* "calls the Jinns and can command them": the man who plays it uses it as the conductor his stick, pointing it to one part or other of the circle where enthusiasm shows signs of fatigue; and as he points it the excitement grows. "And sometimes," says Haila, "a man, or even a woman, gets seized by the Jinn and they will throw off their clothes, and we do not laugh but (putting her fingers to her lips) we say 'thanks be to God, al-hamdu l-Illahi,' and keep silence." But Haila is rather fond of the picturesque.

The visitors at any rate leave after sunset, when the flag is pulled down and the slaves disperse, to gather again later in the evening, and feast on a sheep and dance again.

Cosmetics

Arab and Persian harims are as full of beauty secrets as any other, but the only recipe that seems to have come from them into general European use is that of henna for the hair. The Arab ladies, of course, use it for other things as well—for the beautifying of their nails and palms, and, in places where they go barefoot, for the adornment of their feet, which they paint with henna in the shape of sandals. In Kuwait, where I used to go into these feminine matters with Haila my maid, the latest thing is to paint your nails and finger-tips black and not orange: a very pretty little hand, with the first joints black against the whiteness of the rest looks just as well and no more artificial than our violent red. The stuff they use, said Haila, is called Wasm. She promised to bring me some, and appeared next morning with a bottle of black hair-dye made in Germany, and, presenting it to me with a hopeful glance at my fingers, made me feel what unexpected things our international civilization is capable of.

The washing of my hair opened up another vista of treatments. I could choose either the Kuwaiti town method, which uses the powdered leaf of the *Sidr* tree (*Zyziphus Spina Christi*) like soap: or the Persian fashion, which I know to be excellent, for Jamila, my landlady, used to apply it for me in Baghdad. She got a certain clayey earth, which was laid by for a length of time to acquire a faint perfume, with dried roses: it was then wetted and plastered on the head, with or without henna according to taste, and, washed off after twenty minutes or so, left the hair beautifully smooth and glossy. The earth can be found in many places—anything sufficiently

[137]

clayey seems to do, though that of Kuwait, for instance is not so good as what comes from Qatif, and the very particular get it sent specially by relatives from Persia. The Beduin use it, said Haila—and some will put an egg on first, and the next day smear their hair with butter skimmed and melted and mixed either with saffron powder and rose, or with another scented product called *mahlab*, whose recipe escaped me. In Aden, one can go into little booths of the bazaars and buy all sorts of curious things, lichen from the trees of Frankincense, sea-weed or fish-scales, all to be made up into hair-wash.

The second most important thing in the Arabian toilet is the make-up for the eyes. Black *kohl* is universal, and in the desert is used by men as well as women, very sensibly since it surrounds the eye with coolness and protection in the glare of the sun. The kind that lasts best and looks prettiest is made with cotton stuff wound into a tight wick, burnt to soot and mixed with butter; I have found this recipe on the shores both of the Persian Gulf and the Caspian. Antimony is just as generally used, and is supposed to be better for the eyes though not so becoming: it is imported from the farther East in lumps like silver, left for two or three days in soft, preferably rain water, and scraped off wet in a powder. Sometimes pounded kernels of almonds are mixed in with it, or powdered pearls—a Cleopatra touch.

There are various other kinds of *kohl* known specially to the Beduin—blue *kohl*, or white, used medicinally; and red, also medicinal, made with cochineal and sugar "which we grind with our silver anklets," a woman told me, and often put on the eyes of children to strengthen them.

When the eyes and hair are attended to, very little is done to the rest of the face, and the Arab lady's complexion is apt soon to fade. She uses a sort of pumice stone for the bath or—in Syria—a hard little cake of a substance very like it. In Baghdad the *loofah* plant produces excellent *loofahs* which are sold in the bazaars.

Cosmetics

But for the rest of the make-up, most of the things now used come from Europe. In Kuwait, the eyebrows are still trimmed with a hard wood sent over from the Persian shore, called, generically, *Khatab*, which is said to darken them, though all I could do with mine was to make them a little more glossy by persistent scraping, like the coat of a well-groomed horse.

The teeth are cleaned by the Beduin with a stick of the plant called *hamdh (Salvadora Persica)*, of which they shred the end to make a brush. In Kuwait, however, the Persian ladies use an Indian bark called *dairam*, and press it hard against their lips to make them larger and fuller: the effect lasts for a few days, and then goes bluish—and the rather painful effort has to be repeated: the object is very much that of the early Victorian mother who used to tell her daughters to "bite their lips to make them red when they stepped into a drawing-room."

The object is, indeed, always the same, and has been since the day when Eve first noticed the inadequacy of natural attire. But one can not help wondering that the ladies of the East, having so very little to do otherwise, should not have made more progress in the arts of beauty. It is the busy West which has discovered most of the secrets, and the woman who has come to rely on many other things besides her physical attractions, now comes as an expert in these very matters to her Eastern sister who sits, placidly immured and neglected, meeting old age without resistance.

Built on Sand

When the Italian Governor of Rhodes built his palace, he attended with loving care to every detail, so that the historical tradition of the place might be carried on worthily and no hideous discord shock those who see the new and old together. He went so far as to quarry the stone in its mediæval quarry, so that it might weather like the town behind it and be looked at with pleasure for centuries to come.

One thinks of such things sadly when one looks at the new British Agency in Kuwait.

It is not *badness*, it is the absence of *goodness*, which, in Art as in Life, is so depressing.

Everything about it is just a little wrong.

It embodies the national passion for compromise by being neither a semi-circle, a rectangle, nor a square. The arches which speckle it are dull and similar, unredeemed by that grace of proportion which makes a decoration of monotony. The veranda, which is a pleasant place, gets the sun in summer and the shade in winter. The dining-room fireplace is lined with blue and brown tiles and, in a tropical country, makes one hot to look at. The staircase, which should rise from a cool and noble hall, where the gowns of the desert can sweep with dignity, is—like the road to heaven—an affair of sharp and narrow corners. The redeeming feature, I was told, is solidity—and who ever heard of solidity being desirable in the Bad? Our lumber rooms are still groaning with the indestructible solidity of mid-Victorian furniture.

And if, as is only too probable, this is not the beginning and end of the matter: if Progress, marching hand-in-hand with

Oil, is to erect her palaces over the length and breadth of Arabia, regardless of expense, what may we not fear?

The mind's eye, travelling in the future, sees the shores of the Persian Gulf lined with institutional mansions, homes of Oil Magnates, all modelled on the British Agency in Kuwait. Appalled, we will not linger on this vision, but consider the two possible causes that may make such disasters conceivable.

It is either that we really do not *know* what is lovely when we see it: or that, preserved from the necessity of having to live in it, the India Office, or whoever is ultimately responsible, orders a Government House as ladies in the Wild West order clothes—a measurement or two by post and Providence for the style and fit.

Nothing, one would think, could make an architect more happy than to be given the task of building a palace in an Arabian town. In Kuwait all is ready to his hand—he has only to look about him; the blank walls with wooden gutters and carved spouts, that throw long shadows down the sunlit streets; the long benches beside decorated doors, where little posterns are left for daily traffic; the delicate use of windows; the simple turrets that hold the corners of the palaces, where shafts of wind are caught for summer coolness; the inner courts and carved wooden porticoes and ceilings; the mud-built, pointed archways whose recesses fill the town with patterns of lovely shade. All is there: it needs only the seeing eye and a little of the tradition of Arab architecture elsewhere, to combine these elements into a harmony that will not only fit with its background, but will also produce a house infinitely more comfortable to live in than what is evolved out of the inner consciousness of someone who has never been within some thousand miles of the Persian Gulf and its climate.

We are always criticizing the modern Oriental for the ugliness of his European imitations; Baghdad is filled now with streets of small villas that take all the zest out of one's life while one looks at them; but if we had spent our twenty years there in building something that could be remembered, something that was both beautiful *and* Arabian, it is possible that the modern nationalist might not have had to fall back on the suburban pattern brought him by a young officer from the Caucasus by chance. There is one excellent building in Iraq, and that is the Port buiding in Basra—that and the new English church in Baghdad; otherwise, the glory of the Abbasid arches, their exquisite treatment of brick so well adapted to the stoneless land, their restrained and simple decoration, might just as well never have been, not to speak of older traditions of Babylon or Nineveh! We have ignored it all so completely that it is small wonder if our successors now continue to despise the products of their own land; nor can we blame them if they show a certain lack of discrimination in choosing among the many unsuitabilities of the West.

Meanwhile it is a sad and awful thought to think that the memory of great Empires lives by Architecture in the minds of men. We have done, may long continue to do, as mighty things as any; and if the Romans had built the pipe-line, as the truthful Roman wireless will soon no doubt be saying that they did, some monument would be there yet to make the world remember; as for us, we consider an aluminium tank or two sufficient, being concerned with Dividends rather than immortality.

The 'Ashura

All through the ten days of 'Ashura the Shi'as in Islam mourn
for the death of Husain, until the slow mounting tide of their
grief reaches its climax with the last processions, and the slain
body itself is carried under a bloodstained sheet through wailing crowds, where the red headdress of the Sunni is well advised not to make itself conspicuous. All is represented, every
incident of the fatal day of Kerbela; and the procession stops
at intervals to act one episode or other in a little clearing of
the crowd. One can hear it coming from far away by the thud
of the beaters beating their naked chests, a mighty sound like
the beating of carpets; or see the blood pour down the backs
of those who acquire merit with flails made of knotted chains
with which they lacerate their shoulders, bared for the purpose: and when the body itself comes, headless (the man's
head is hidden in a box and a small boy with a fan walks
beside it to prevent suffocation), its two feet sticking out of
the bloody drapery, the truncated neck of a sheep protruding
at the other end, a dagger cunningly stuck above each shoulder into the cloth—when this comes heaving through the
crowd, there is such a passion of anger and sorrow, such a
wailing of women from the roofs, such glances of repulsion
towards the foreigner who happens to be looking on, that it is
quite understandable that the civilized governments of the
East are now doing all they can to discourage this expression
of religion in favour of forms more liturgical.

Kuwait being a Sunni town, where the Persians have come
in numbers during recent years only, there is no procession
there to disturb the dignity of Arab behaviour with orgies of

emotion: but the people have their own little wailing gatherings in the privacy of various houses, and the women have theirs as well as the men, and come back feeling—as one's nurse used to say—"all the better for a good cry" and with the glow of virtue as well.

We had Persian friends in Kuwait who said they would disguise us in abbas and take us. We went accordingly and sat chatting of this and that with an innocent air till the grandfather departed and left us—a bigoted old man who objected to anyone of his family leaving the Harim at all: once clothed for the street, however, no one could possibly tell his own daughter from another: we had a long black chiffon *thaub* trailing about our ankles, its ample sleeve drawn like a hood above our head and covering the face. A black wool abba over the forehead, with sleeves hanging loose about the shoulders, satisfied that innate Oriental instinct for using things in ways which they were never intended to be used; it is simply not done in Kuwait, or Baghdad either for that matter, to put your arms into the sleeve of your abba: what one does is to hold it tight under the chin so that one eye and the nose are covered. This leaves one eye to deal with the traffic of the street, and one hand for all the rest of one's floating draperies: sandals that stick by the big toe only, we felt unequal to on this occasion, and clung to our own slippers with heels: and so hidden, sallied forth into the world—which was a half-deserted street deep in dust—and followed our hostess with some anxiety, fearing that if we once took our eyes off, we should never be able to distinguish her again from any passing female.

She led us through an unassuming door into a porch, whence already a devotional babel could be heard. But we were not to walk simply in. They funked it at the last, and decided to lead us a devious way, up a ladder by the neighbouring roof to a secluded little stair whose lower end the friendly mistress of the house had considerably blocked with tubs of washing, a barricade between us and the religious gathering immediately below. This was an excellent arrangement, except for the difficulty of climbing an unsafe ladder with one eye only and all those clothes, in full view of the surrounding roofs: we did it, however, and found ourselves in a perfect position for seeing, with a sheltered part of stair where, when the heat became unbearable, we could return for a moment and throw our abbas off our faces and breathe.

The heat down below must have been appalling, but no one seemed to mind. There was already a solid floor of squatting women. More kept on arriving all the time, stumbling from hand to hand till they divested themselves of the veil which hid their faces. They were all in black for mourning, with no gold, their hands and hair unadorned with henna, their faces brown and drab as the breasts where babies in bright caps— the only points of colour—lay sucking here and there. Some smoked a hookah; all talked; a few leading spirits busied themselves among them with aluminium kettles of pale tea, moving about with philanthropic uninterested amiability which reminded me of vicarage garden parties.

Otherwise the atmosphere was not a bit like a garden party, or a vicarage either. It was a small court, with two pointed arches at one end, of whitewashed mud and straw, roughly decorated. Old awnings prolonged the shade in patches half across the open space, and at the upper end, under the twilight of the arches, black cloth was nailed around with little squares of cardboard in sign of mourning. Here, with a green satin banner behind them, stood the four ladies who conducted the ceremony, chanting their parts, repeating one line over and over before they went on to the next, and bobbing with every verse to the congregation, which rose and bobbed in return like a wave, diminishing toward the outer distance.

One wondered, as one watched, into what dim prehistoric days this monotonous chant might lead one, back and back through the recesses of time. The four Readers, unconscious of being observed, stood as if drugged with dull pain while they beat their breasts. They were all different in type—the nearest handsome like a Roman matron, very white under the black double kerchief of the Iraq headdress, which tied her brows like a crown. She had let down a piece of her bodice, and a triangle of white skin showed, slowly growing red and angry under the constant limp beat of her podgy, grubby little hand, black-rimmed round the finger-nails. Besides her was a dark slave-type whose African blood shows hysterically under stress of emotion. She had a huge mouth, and thin and waving arms, and her thumbs stuck out and showed the paler inner side of the palms: she did not beat her breast, but thumped hard on the little red note-book where her part was written, with an energy which made one realize how deeply the idea of Vicarious Punishment must be embedded in human nature. Next her stood a very Persian type, close-lipped, with regular features and straight brows; and beyond, a young cow-like woman, double-chinned, amiable and absent-minded, who had to refer to her note-book at frequent intervals. As they thumped their breasts the congregation thumped with them, and the thick mud walls of the court answered dully to the sound: sometimes the attention slackened; little private con-versations sprang up here and there—a special plaintive note from the pulpit was required to get things going again. And presently, after a rest—for the recitation had been going on for an hour or more, and the leaders had changed at inter-vals—they draped one half of their heads in their black gowns and took black silk veils trailing in their hands: the metre changed from the staccato trochaic to a wailing anapæstic measure: real weeping shook the crowd. In the alcove, behind the arches out of sight, candles were lit; a little procession came in with trays on its head—a tray covered with a green-edged brocade, magenta and silver; four behind it with can-dles—five or seven on each—pink and white sweets, and a saucer of henna; and a last tray with a jug of water, green

lettuce, salt and pepper. As they were borr
ers reached the ecstasy of their sorrow: t'
the death of Husain: they turned to righ
of the women followed them as they turn
the trays, weeping too, tilted them and their
angles; until, in a scrimmage, the lights disappeared a.
sweets were scattered, every sweet or candle being able to give
to its possessor the fulfilment of her wish.

Before the excitement of this climax had subsided we left
our places, climbed to our roof, and came away, for curious
glances had already been cast towards us. And as we walked
back, closely veiled through the dusty street, I thought, not of
this violence of passion, but of the august ritual of our own
cathedrals, æthereal and remote; and wondered in what sim-
ilarity of instinct, what selfsame desire to express the inex-
pressible in visible shape, this too had had its birth. On the
last day of the 'Ashura the Persian children in Kuwait are
taken to the Mulla, who passes a knife under their chin in sign
of sacrifice or dedication; from mythology to religion, from
religion to mysticism, the great truths pass: and it is well now
and then to see them in those simple forms that belong to our
first awakening in this world, so that we may not forget the
brotherhood of men.

One of the Four Holy Cities of Iraq

A VISIT TO THE SHRINE AT KADHIMAIN

I had been in the holy city of Kadhimain as tourist, with an anxious policeman watching to see what we did not carelessly brush the sacred threshold with the hem of our garments, while a hostile crowd of Shi'as, chiefly either Persian or of Persian descent, stood around to watch. It was an unsatisfactory way of doing it, and I told my friend Nuri that I would like to go one day in a less conspicuous manner. Christians are never allowed in, but I would go during the Ramadhan fast in the evening, for the shine is then kept open till late at night, and the dim lighting would make things easier. Nuri had Shi'a friends in the Holy City willing to take me; and I would go to them with two of his sisters, taking the tram from Baghdad together with the other pilgrims.

Accordingly, as the dusk was falling one evening along the river, Nuri came for me with a bundle of black clothes—a small chiffon veil called a Pushi to tie over one's head, and an abba draped across the forehead and shoulders so that the empty sleeveholes fall like wings and the whole thing covers one up like a cape. In one of the blind river alleys which are conveniently numerous I slipped these garments on, and reappeared on the deserted "bund" as like a Baghdadi as anyone could wish. I had taken the trouble to beautify my eyes with a thick black line of kohl, so that I could throw back the veil when men were not about, and, holding the cloak to my mouth, could look around me. As we reached the lights and traffic of the Maude bridge, I pulled the veil modestly down and stood while Nuri went for a cab, and looked around at the twilight world in which I had enveloped myself with a strange sensation of having become suddenly disembodied. English friends, going to and fro to their dinners in cars, looked straight through me. With hesitating steps, for I could not well see what I was treading on, I crossed over to the cab, while a policeman waved his arm, impatient with the uncertain progress of Arab ladies, whose difficulties I was now sympathizing with to the full.

We jostled through narrow streets and dark bazaars; came to a small door in a blank wall; knocked and were drawn in like conspirators to where the two sisters, ready veiled, stood waiting; and presently, with advice and good wishes, and a small maid carrying a lantern before us, we sallied forth to the tram.

I never saw this venerable relic by day. By night it looked like some huge machine which, having got rusted over in the deluge, creaked ever since. It was drawn by horses along rails. It had two carriages, one for men and one for women—the latter, when we settled in it, full of stout negresses from whose overflowing garments unexpected babies rolled out and tumbled. In the dim light one could just see the white-rimmed eyes and bits of black cheeks and noses, for they kept their faces covered.

We jangled out among the courts and houses. A candle in a dirty lantern swayed from the roof, scattering grease. The ticket collector came, his head swathed in a check cloth, as if for toothache; from our black folds we produced the slips of paper, which he took to read in the centre of the carriage one by one, waiting for a favourable lurch of the candle for light to punch them by.

And now we had left the suburbs of Karkh, the old city of Mansur. We were out under the stars, with shapes of palm trees moving against the blue night sky. And suddenly, as if standing alone in space, the tops of the four gilt minarets of the Holy City appeared, illuminated by the lights at their summits which shine through all the nights of Ramadhan. A row of small green and red and yellow lights below enclosed the square of the shrine: the two golden domes gleamed here and there, almost invisible in the shadow of the night. The deep sky behind, the half-lighted building, the carriage full of pilgrims in their dim abstraction, had a strange solemnity: the surrounding darkness hid all the ugliness and squalor which ever comes near beauty in the East. We rumbled to a standstill, climbed down the ladder-like steps of the Father of Trams, and with some difficulty in following the directions, finally reached the house of our Shi'a friends.

Here we stepped into the twentieth century. The master of the house was an engineer who had travelled in Egypt: his young brother, in a béret and very baggy flannels, studied law in Alexandria: and his wife, who was also coming with us, had shingled hair and a little French headdress under her veil. They had no misgivings, they said, so long as I did not speak, for my accent would betray me. They had taken Christians into the shrine before, but no Europeans, though several European women have been inside at one time and another. We drank coffee and ate sweetmeats, and presently set forth with a servant and lantern ahead to light the gaping pitfalls of the street; for we had left the twentieth century again, and were moving under dark overhanging houses into the dark bazaar. Dim figures, squatting silent by their closed booths, with rosaries over their idle fingers, peered at us passing; the shadowy gate and its high threshold, where in the daytime so many jealous faces had prevented our approach, now stood before us, the entrance to a world incredibly unchanged and old.

We crossed the threshold under a looped chain that one touches, for it confers a blessing, into the great court or piazza of the sanctuary. It seemed enormously spacious: the whole constellation of Orion hung above it in black depths of sky.

One of the Four Holy Cities of Iraq

Round three sides are porticoes faced with flowered tiles. The lights above and the light from the clock shed a pleasant twilight in which many gowned figures paced up and down. A group in a corner held a newspaper: the Holy Cities, and the mosques more especially, are great places for the hatching of seditions. Black groups of women sat about on the pavement. The space is so wide that numbers can walk here and there without making it look crowded. In an absurd way I thought of the square of St. Mark's on a summer evening.

And now we came to a gilt porch on slim wooden columns, the outer door of the shrine itself. A man crouching there took our shoes and added them to others in rows. I had just advanced to enter under the heavy curtain, when a Sayid in green turban, one of the descendants of the Prophet, called me back, giving me a very unpleasant shock. One of my companions clutched at my abba with a shaking hand: the Sayid, however, was only calling us because he knew our host and wished to do us honour. "You belong to the House," he told him. "I myself will take you round."

And so, as we stood on the step before the heavy curtain, he called the blessing upon us—of 'Ali and Muhammad and the two Imams of their family—in a voice so beautiful, chanting its invocation in the night air for us who were about to enter the sanctuary, that I have rarely heard anything more impressive and more appealing. "Allah is great," he said, and motioned us to enter.

We first came into a gallery roofed with stalactite work of mirrors, glittering dimly, and with mirrors let into cheap and bad woodwork round the sides: and then coming to another curtain between very tall double doors of beaten silver, with thin models of the hand of 'Abbas cut out in silver sheets and nailed across the design here and there—we stepped into the inner sanctuary of the tomb.

It was a very high room with two great silver doorways at right angles to each other. Glass chandeliers in numbers hung from the ceiling. The walls were adorned with arabesques in colours on a dark ground. On the floor were carpets poor in quality. All this was but the setting for the tomb.

It stood in the middle within its triple cage, whose outer silver more than half-way up is constantly polished by the hands and the lips of the faithful, passing in endless procession. The bars of beaten silver worked in patterns are like window gratings framed in pointed arches, so that the tomb looks as if it had five windows on the longer and three on the shorter side. It must be about ten feet high. The top is decorated with horizontal mouldings to soften the uncompromising squareness, and surmounting all are the little green flags of the house of 'Ali.

If you stand at the grating, with your face pressed against the silver bars, you see dimly, through another grating of iron and through a case of glass, the two carved wooden coffins of the Imams. To do this, people will walk from Afghanistan and India and the remotest provinces of Persia. Swarthy bearded men were here, and almost hairless Mongolian faces; the lean drooping Persian, and flat-faced Shi'a of Iraq. Sitting in complete abstraction before great leaden candlesticks on the ground, pilgrims with heavy turbans chanted the holy verses, swaying softly. Women were in one corner, murmuring together in their black draperies on the floor. I followed the Sayid, pressing my hands against the bars, moving slowly from right to left round the tomb. A woman beside me sobbed desperately, and kissed the polished silver, and pressed her hands to every knob she could reach. Thousands, millions of these hands pass over that indifferent surface smoothing it away with their hopes and prayers, the piteous faith of mankind.

In that room the very atmosphere was electric with emotion. One could not stand there without feeling the passion of it, its utter completeness, its ancient cruelty behind that quiet calm of prayer, behind those figures standing with upturned palms and faces, lost in their ecstasy. An alien discovered here, I reflected, would scarcely reach the outer gateway; and then there would be the bazaar, and what a nasty mess for the police. My little friend ahead of me was still trembling, hurrying through her pilgrimage with rather unseemly haste. This was not the atmosphere even for the Westernized Oriental: this was the Old East, incompatible with all we bring and do: it was they or us, and they would have a right to murder us if they found us, here where the old law held.

We had reached the short side of the tomb, farthest from the door. The Sayid again chanted a prayer, while we stood with upturned palms: again the beauty of the words, the passion of devotion all around me, made me forget that I was a stranger: there is but one accent of faith, after all.

We made our way slowly down the fourth side. Instead of the five window patterns, the centre is here taken up by what appears to be the entrance to the tomb, all in beaten silver, but square instead of having the pointed finish of the other decoration. I could not ask, being afraid to speak.

Luckily, as we were women, it was not our business to thank the Sayid. Our host did so, while we slipped into the court to the Keeper of Shoes, who beats the Savoy cloakroom attendant, for he gave us our own pairs without a word of explanation, though he could see nothing except our shapeless silhouettes and the cotton stocking which I had allowed to droop over my ankle to make it look more genuinely like female Baghdad.

As we stood there a water carrier came up, dressed in a short tunic to the thighs, his pointed jar hung by a strap across his shoulders and a brass saucer in his hand. "Water of the Way. The water that was refused to our lord Husain on the Day of Kerbela." I paid four annas like the rest, and wondered if I committed a sacrilege by pouring away the water, for the public bowl was used by too many sick and maimed to be tempting. Nothing was said. We stepped out of the secret enclosure, over the high threshold, under the chain, into the dark bazaar. Our tram, clanking like Juggernaut, took us back through the starlight: we had a last view of the golden domes: the four minarets and their lights shone clear and still against the midnight sky.

Samarra and Tekrit

One of the pleasantest bodies of men in Iraq are the police. They get from £2 to £3 a month, their uniform, boots, arms and food. They seem always smart and cheerful. They are the traveller's refuge in every sort of trouble, from a flood to a hold-up, and provide him with every sort of necessity, from postage stamps to lodgings for the night. The solitary police-less traveller they regard with solicitude after sunset, and otherwise with that friendly tolerance which the East reserves for lunatics or idiots, afflicted by God.

We set out peacefully for Samarra, for the road is now safe as houses, whatever that may mean: but when we decided to go on to Tekrit the morning after and see the birthplace of Saladin, a policeman leaped in beside us and provided agreeable conversation for the rest of the day, and so brought it into my mind to begin this essay with a well-earned outpouring of praise for the police in general. We, however, set forth unchaperoned, and took the north road from Baghdad through Kadhimain, and, being three women on our own, unhampered by that worry about their dignity which embitters the lives of men, found everybody friendly and lingered at every coffee hut to take photographs and talk with travelling shepherds resting beside low doors in scraps of shade. They gave a pastoral air to a landscape which provides nothing in the way of vegetation but small inedible shrubs on flat stretches of clay soil; but they come from farther away—seven days or so with their sheep to the Baghdad market—and it was a group of these men who told us to see Tekrit, and to ask there for the descendants of the Christian Abd as-Satih, who leaped his mare from the high cliff into the Tigris and was drowned rather than submit to Islam.

The Arab has a respect for the written word which must come down from ages of magic, and the shepherds pulled a red note-book from their tattered gowns and asked us to write our names to commemorate our meeting. We left them, and after another stretch of clay, strewn here and there with potsherds of vanished habitations, saw men of the Shammar marching from the north beside their camels, from whose high swaying framework the women look down with glints of silver anklet or turquoise nose-ring. We knew the Shammar, and promised to visit their Shaikh near Balad on our return and, driving through the village, sunk in garden walls and cornfields, came by another empty stretch to the river's edge and the ferry.

Here flocks were being brought across in a flat-bottomed shahtur. They were gathered in groups at the foot of the low mud cliff opposite, like vine-clusters: below them, the hovels of east Balad jut into the stream, scarce distinguishable from the mud-flats which generate them: above, the uninhabited river flows in a wide and empty bed by empty islands; small grey whirlpools eddy down the flood, turning on their own axis like the solar system; the prehistoric flat barge, crowded with sheep with their heads down, came slowly, urged by plank-like oars; and over the whole scene, in its flatness and leisure, lay that singular peacefulness, that desert enchantment made of Loneliness and Time.

One of my ideas of happiness is to sit on a river bank waiting for a ferry. It is much pleasanter than dinner parties, which are spoilt by the fact that one has to think of more than one thing at once. Two donkeys agreed with me, or would have if they knew what dinner parties are. They stood head to tail, and practised collective security by flicking the flies off each other's noses in a mute and happy companionship independent of the labours of conversation. A woman from Balad stood waiting also, swathed in black with tattooed lips; she took proffered slices of the oranges we were eating and wrapped them carefully in her long sleeve for her sick child. She stooped to the stream to pick up the rind which we had carelessly cast away; it also she kept to take home, saying that "the scent is good." There is not much riches in Balad.

The shahtur came stranding downstream beside us, like a large punt. The sheep huddled out while our car clanked on; the donkeys, the woman, two peasants and ourselves settled round it; and the men of Balad, pulling from the prow, sang as they rowed.

"We poured out to our enemies death" (murr, they called it, bitterness).

"We poured out to our enemies *death*." The pull came with the final word.

The master of the shahtur gave a new verse:

"The Turkish bullet flies *fast*." With the sixth verse we neared the opposite bank. The waiting woolly mass of sheep rolled towards us; their shepherds made gurgling noises to ask them to wait till we landed: and in less than half an hour over the flat East-Tigris lands, we had Samarra and its golden dome in sight.

It is the most Arab and least Persian of the four Holy Cities, enclosed in walls in an arid belt of ruins that overhang on a low cliff the garden oasis of riverlands below. It is clean and friendly and, completely surrounded and much used by the nomads, has lost some of that misanthropic feeling towards the outer world characteristic of Iraqi towns, the result of many vicissitudes, mostly unpleasant.

Samarra had one brief period of splendour, of less than fifty years: eight caliphs built or beautified successive palaces; and the stuccos, unique and lovely, with which they wainscoted their rooms are now being gradually unearthed to adorn the new Arab museum in Baghdad.

There is no European in the town, but three Iraqi archæologists were furthering the work of culture on their own with a zest and enthusiasm delightful to anyone except possibly the pedantically trained expert. We found them charming. What more fascinating game than to be given a city of ruins twenty-eight miles long to play about with and a little money to do it? They had unearthed the base of the cone-shaped tower and their men were crawling up like caterpillars in long lines, renovating the spiral staircase to the top. They had propped the outer walls of the great mosque beside it, and took us wandering through the latest of their palaces, with the stuccos still in position round their labyrinth of rooms. Here we paused, to discuss with the workmen where the next site should be, in a friendly vociferous manner which made one think of the arguments of Odysseus with his crew. After some waving of shovels, the site was chosen; the assembled workmen performed a little dance for our benefit as we stood in the uncovered rooms below—their picks and shovels raised and lowered like spears against the skyline—they gave a last wave and wandered off to their new site and lunch while the water-boys picked up the heavy oozing yellow jars and followed. Our host, slight, ascetic and gentle, with grey hair waved back from his forehead amd European clothes, led us back, expounding shyly, to where, over cups of tea, in a court with flowering pomegranate trees and low rooms built around it, his two companions took up the tale. There was something pleasantly restful about this archæology; no clash of theory, no horrid criticism of people whose only crime is that they think differently about things that happened ever so long ago; all one does in Samarra is just to go and dig and produce objects out of the ground. Sir Henry Layard would have felt at home here. So did we. One thing only troubled us. Some time during the Middle Ages, the lower part of the spiral tower and great mosque provided bricks for the building of the wall of what was then new Samarra. People went and took what they could reach, eating away the foundations of their ancient monuments in the recognized Eastern way, till the upper structure threatened to topple on their heads; now, say the archæologists, the bricks are to be taken back to where they came from, and the wall of Samarra is being demolished to the consternation of its inhabitants.

The inhabitants are in a fix, since the Government of Iraq prides itself on a state of security which renders all walls superfluous; to say that a wall may come in useful later on, is like advising a rich uncle about his investments—it suggests he may not live for ever. So the inhabitants of Samarra lament in private and say nothing. The bricks are quite ordinary bricks, made—to our untutored eyes—exactly like the bricks they make to-day; and Samarra without its walls will be a dingy-looking place; so that if this page ever happens to fall under the eye of someone with power to do so, I hope he will yet stretch out his hand to save the mediæval wall of Samarra and allow the Abbaside structures to be restored with materials slightly less chronological.

For my own part, not being an archæologist, I like ruins merely as places to sit about and think in; and one can usually do that much better before anyone has been scratching in the earth. A certain minimum is necessary, just as in religion—something of a peg for the imagination to clothe; but when it comes to catalogues and labels, the charm is snapped.

And so, in the afternoon, we drove to the untouched northern end of Samarra and there, in the twilight of a dust storm, stood in the mosque court of Abu Dilaf, and saw its broken piers gather immensity, like a Stonehenge around us in the declining light. We had driven for miles along the undeviating straightness of the buried highway, with mounds of houses, straight shapeless ridges, on either hand, and streets running into it outlined also by low, almost obliterated mounds. So New York, ruined and rectilinear, may look in the fullness of time. This place was once loud with the brawls of Turkish Prætorians; caliph after caliph was murdered; intrigue and

violence walked the streets perpetually: now, on the borders
of its loneliness, blue-headed thistles stand like little crucifixes
with arms outspread, in endless rows along the edges of the
mounds. The drab disc of sun, round and small like a moon,
scarce shone through the scudding dust. In the ruins of the
great court two jays flitted with brilliant elusive wings, under
the dust-coloured colonnade, against the dust-coloured sky,
and reminded us that out of this drab material, Life itself, so
vivid and various, may spring at any time.

The caliphs of Samarra, in the course of their rapid and
unfortunate career, added one more to the religious complications of Islam by causing the disappearance of the 12th
Imam, Ja'far the Truthful, and so provided the Shi'as with
that invaluable asset, a Hidden Leader liable at any moment
to become incarnate.

The prison where he was last seen is now enshrined, together with the tombs of the 10th and 11th Imams immediately preceding, under two domes of the sanctuary whose
blank walls and four doorways form the centre of the town.
A market street runs before it, with coffee benches ranged
along the walls; and in one of the side streets, dusty and
tortuous, under an arched doorway of carved brickwork, a
lodging had been prepared for us in the house which the
Rajah of Pirpur keeps for the use of pilgrims. Shaikh Sa'id, in
abba and green turban, was waiting to receive us.

He had prepared beds in a room which looked through
open arches on to a portico of carved wooden pillars, three
feet or so above the level of the little court. It was an inner
court, the harim of the house, entered by an only door from
the men's outer apartments, and perfectly private since the
house was now uninhabited. Against one of the pillars a huge,
slim-waisted, long-beaked copper vessel full of water was
brought for our use. An old Caucasian, stranded in Samarra
by the war, was left to shamble about in slippers and minister
to our needs. He seemed morose till I tried him in Persian,

when his face suddenly dislocated itself into innumerable wrinkles and he began to talk, and told us of his sorrow, marooned in a land with not a hill in sight. His own country, where he had brothers living, was unattainable, having become Russian since the war. There is no Russian minister in Iraq, and no one else could provide a passport, and so the years passed and he lived on in Samarra, dreaming of hills and streams. Once only had he gone to Baghdad to be cured of some illness, had gone unavailingly to see the Persian consul there, and realizing the difficulties before him, elderly and without influence, had resigned himself and returned where the people were kind to him in their quiescent way, an exile by the will of God.

His story gave to our peace that tinge of sadness which nearly always goes with peace in the East, coming as it does either before or after some sort of a catastrophe. It is a quietude both deeper and more precarious than that of the West, which we used to be rather apt to take lightly for granted. In Samarra we enjoyed it, and thought favourably of harims when one can have them to oneself.

In the evening, preceded by round trays full of supper carried on people's heads, Shaikh Sa'id came to eat with us; we feasted on *pilau* and delicious preserves sticky with sugar; Sayyids of the shrine and city elders came to call; and at last we slept, safe and protected in our open court, since our host, out of his hospitality, seeing that we were women and alone, left his own house and camped where he could guard us, in the men's apartment between the harim and the street.

TEKRIT

Apart from our meeting with the shepherds and their story of Abd as-Satih, I had wished for years to reach Tekrit, and seeing it on the map only forty miles north of us, had suggested a visit. S. and Peggy however, take a more enlightened interest in ruins than I do, and were reluctant to be drawn from Samarra, till we discovered that there was no ferry across to the ruins of the western bank. There is no bridge over the Tigris all the way between Baghdad and Mosul; when the river rises communications are apt to be interrupted by the flooding of the lower lands, and the popularity of government here will depend on whether or no Samarra gets a bridge. Meanwhile we had either to return to Balad or drive north to the ferry of Tekrit and thence downstream upon the western ruins; and having naturally decided to do this we started off with a policeman beside us, and began the day in the happiest orthodox manner with a puncture just beyond the town.

There is nothing like this early, almost inevitable puncture to put one into that adaptable and leisurely frame of mind essential to enjoyment in the East.

The day was fine. Malwiya, the great tower, stood squat in a sky filled, it seemed, with little white shining particles of light. A shepherd boy was reaping corn in a small hollow, a pocket of moisture, evidently, in the unwatered barrenness of the rest of the landscape. He had a round, half-moon sickle with three rings jingling loose upon the handle, meant—he said—to make a pleasant noise for the reaper. Charmed with something so non-utilitarian, we watched him. Sometimes the reapers here have metal finger-tips with long talons for their left hand to grasp the ears—but this little patch was scarce big enough for anything so professional. The lad squatted and cut his handfuls slowly; his sheep drifted behind, cropping in the stubble, never thinking of trespassing; until in the fulness of time our car came up, with the policeman waving cheerfully inside it.

He was a big featureed, green-eyed man called Rashid, a Kurd and a Sunni, "though it is better now to call oneself Iraqi rather than Kurd"; and he was the most open, outspoken, good-natured grown up boy one can imagine. The *inscrutability* of the East is, indeed, I believe a myth; the only inscrutable object I know in Iraq is the British Embassy, which devotes itself to physical culture in super-Oriental seclusion: the ordinary inhabitant is incomprehensible merely to people who never trouble to have anything much to do with him.

Rashid, however, came more than half-way to meet us. Perhaps it was the prospect of a day out which bubbled so happily inside him. When we passed a few Beduin women with black draperies fluttering in the wind beside a desert well: "There you see them—dogs, children of dogs," he said, turning himself towards us with a perfectly irresistible smile that split his face from ear to ear. "Nobody gives us the trouble that these give us. There you see them, so polite you say they are kings—and you don't know whom they may just have murdered in their tents—and how is one to find out? One goes and asks: 'Where is so and so?' and they tell you he is in some tent out of sight, days away, or ill inside with the women—and all the while they have him there buried. Dogs," he repeated, catching some murmur of protest, for we are all friends of the Beduin; "they give us more trouble than an army of enemies. And you can never get them together—one here, one there, their houses far out of sight of each other and moving all the time. All day we ride about because of them." He smiled as if it were a greater joke than ever. "And their women," he added in a lower voice, as if it were almost incredible and something of a secret, "their women are worse, if that is possible, than the men."

We had run past Dura, the site of Julian's battle, and—ever keeping along the edges of buried ruins in this cemetery of a land—now turned sharp down towards the green corn flats that face Tekrit across the Tigris.

No one who comes upon this magnificent position can fail to realize what an important place it must ever have been in days of insecurity. It used to be counted the last town of Iraq and lifts itself out of the flatness of that alluvial land in a series of high cliffs, sheer from the river. Our troops discovered it, marching from Baghdad, and occupied and built hutments along the northern heights. They must have unearthed a good many Islamic fragments, digging their way upstream from Samarra; their zig-zag trenches chose the vantage point of every ancient mound. Now, scarce altered by twenty years in the uncultivated land, empty under the sun, they commemorate more sharply then words the desolate remoteness of that long campaign.

South of the old British camp, divided by a deep ravine, is mediæval Tekrit, a Christian town in the tenth century, with a monastery, and surrounded, when Ibn Jubayr visited it in A.D. 1184, by towers and walls three miles or more in circuit. Fragments of the boulders that underpinned the cliff still cling to its overhanging sides, a brick pier of the old gateway near the water's edge, and caverns and debris of masonry in the hillside. The top is pitted with shallow holes, where the inhabitants dig illicitly for antiques by night: and that is all that remains of their ancient Christian magnificence, except the legend of Abd as-Satih and the fact that the present Moslemized inhabitants still keep up a traditional relationship with the Christians of al-Kosh, a village north of Mosul.

We remembered our conversation with the shepherds, and soon mentioned the name of the local hero, whereupon a drab and rather unheroic-looking young man disentangled himself from a small promiscuous crowd and told us that his name was Thuwaini, and Abd as-Satih was "one of his grandfathers," and that they had been two brothers, with strongholds on the Tigris and Euphrates. That was all he knew, a nebulous story once no doubt clothed with life when the Byzantine citizens struggled against the enveloping forces of Islam; or perhaps it represents some later dealing with minorities, drastically modern, now lost in the unrecorded bloodshed of mediæval Iraq.

We left these meditations, and descended by the southern ravine to the present town, which covers a lower hill and is

full of charming windows carved in brick-work patterns, and
pretty women who still carry earthenware jars on their shoulders down to their little beach on the Tigris edge. What we
however were looking for was our car, and having found that,
our policeman, whom we discovered in the dimness of a coffee shed on the edge of the town, his engaging smile half
buried in a bowl of soup. It was lunch time; the soup smelt
good, full of lentils and pieces of mutton in a rich juice; we
took an outer table and joined Tekrit at its meal, and paid
sixpence for the three of us; and in the afternoon travelled
downstream by the western road—past the Shrine of the
Forty, a dull little solitary sanctuary—to the hill where the
ruins of the Lover's Castle still look across the Tigris to Samarra.

It, too, is crossed and surrounded by trenches half fallen in,
and as we descended to Samarra railway station to drop our
policeman there, we passed a small black-railed cemetery
where British troops lie buried.

"So many dead in this land," I remarked, rendered a trifle
melancholy no doubt by two consecutive days of ruins.

"And killed what for? For nothing," said S., who has two
sons just growing up into this uncomfortable world.

Our policeman, who had fallen rather silent except when
the sight of a stray Beduin roused his hunting instincts, now
turned round with more vehemence than we had seen in him.

"You must not say they were killed for nothing," he said.
"What do we live for, if not the words that are spoken of us
when we die? These men were killed honourably. After their
death all their people praised them." He flattened out one
hand before him and made a show as if to write upon it with
the other. "We live for what is written by our deeds."

Good man. Here was no Press-made propaganda. He spoke
his faith naturally. We reached the cross-roads and stopped
while he gathered his rifle.

"Our people have given you Iraq as a present," I said, still thinking of the cemetery and the trenches in the desert. "I hope you won't forget it too soon."

The police are not supposed to take money, and I have never been able to make them do so. He brushed our little gift aside, smiled and shook hands and left us, his square khaki shoulders, strong boots and smart puttees strangely solid in the indefinite landscape. And I think of him now and then, riding with some companion, two by two as one sees them along the desert roads, "writing," as he said, "his life by his deeds."

Nejf

We sat in a little circle, seven effendis, the Rais Baladiya, and myself, on chairs on the quayside at Kufa, at the northern end of the town. Its one line of houses, small quay, and moored barges with painted blue trellis-work cabins, were foreshortened, and vague in the dusk. Sucking up to the bank with a gurgle now and then, as if to join in the conversation, the Euphrates flowed at our feet, wide in flood. The shaving of a new moon appeared above it, declaring the end of Safar, the second month of mourning; and at the sign of its straw-coloured crescent, a dozen fires or more shone in the palm-tree darkness of the opposite bank: they flickered up and down, waved by unseen arms, and then drifted for a second or two, burning, downstream: they are thrown in at the end of the month of lamentation to carry away the sorrows of the year, a custom no doubt as ancient as the river-made land itself. Our modern Iraqis, dressed European, their sidaras on their laps, seeing these flames, glanced up at the crescent *hillal*, and wished each other luck, as unconscious of moon worship as the average churchgoing Englishman when he sings *Halleluiah*.

It seemed right that the pagan worship should remain on the far eastern bank, where the tomb of Ezekiel and the tower of Babel still stand as landmarks of a world submerged. But as you cross the bridge of boats to Kufa you step from Babilonia into the history of Islam. Between it and Nejf lies, destroyed under the sand, the Arab capital of the Kings of Hira. The shrunken modern town of Kufa is surrounded on three sides by sandy hillocks where the Beduin conquerors' town lies buried. The great mosque where Ali was murdered as he prayed still stands, empty except in a time of pilgrims; and remnants of Ali's house, under a small blue dome. The castle, they say, was destroyed by the Ummayyad, Abd al-Malik ibn Marwan. As he sat there in his diwan he heard an old Beduin murmur: "You will be the fifth."

"What fifth?" said the King.

"When I first came to Kufa," the old Beduin replied, "I saw the head of Husain between the hands of Obaidallah his murderer. I went away, and when I next came to Kufa, I saw the head of Obaidallah between the hands of al-Mukhtar ibn Yusuf who killed him. I went away, and when I next came I saw the head of al-Mukhtar between the hands of Mus'ab ibn Zubair. I went away, and now I have returned, and I see the head of Mus'ab ibn Zubair in your hands."

And Abd al-Mahik left Kufa and had the castle destroyed, which is now a ruin close to the house of Ali.

No legend could bring the life and character of old Kufa more vividly before one. Less a city than a camp, spearhead of the nomad advance against the settled lands, the desert waves seem to break against this shore in a foam of blood. Ali here, made for gentler things, wore his life out, sick at heart among the fickle townsmen: and it was not far from here that Husain his son was met and turned away with his pathetic band, and left to wander up Euphrates towards the desert place of Kerbela.

There he pitched his camp, while his enemies surrounded him and held the water: the details are as living to-day as then, 1,257 years ago; nor can anyone with much profit visit these Holy Cities unless he knows something of the story, for its tragedy is built into their very foundations. It is one of the few stories I can never read without weeping. It has come down with the inevitability, the slow growth of Doom, of a Greek tragedy, and with the human pathos of living people humanly beloved.

Nejf

An offer of amnesty was made and refused by every one of the little band of relatives and companions: a last day's respite was given; the last night came and, in Husain's tent, while his servant sat singing burnishing his sword, his sister Zeinab came to say farewell—that same Zeinab who, later with the other women to Damascus, is buried in a beautiful Kufic tomb in the Maidan with Shi'a and Sunni graves around her and sixteen of the severed heads of Kerbela.

Then, in the morning, a moment of stillness fell on the surrounding army. The first arrow was shot. The slow, heartrending process of the day is told. Fought to a finish, it ended in the death of every one of the small band (every combatant is said to have been beheaded after the battle and seventy only were counted), and the last scene comes as the head of Husain is laid before Obaidallah in Kufa, and as he spurns it with his foot, an old man's voice in the crowd is heard to say: "Deal gently with it, for by God, many a time have I seen those lips kissed by the blessed lips of Muhammad."

History has stopped since that day in Kerbela and Nejf: they live on their memory of hate.

I drove between them one day along the desert strip in a rather derelict taxi and tried to save the lives of huge lizards who tramp there in large numbers with clumsy, scaly steps and often end like Diehards under the Wheels of Progress. The taxi-driver liked running over them, and when I remarked they were, after all, harmless, said: "No. They creep up to a flock of sheep from behind and suck the udders of the ewes without their noticing."

I persisted, however, and presently asked the name of a solitary dome among the distant trees.

"That," said the driver, "is the sanctuary of Al-Hurr."

Al-Hurr was the Arab chief sent to turn Husain from Kufa, whose courteous behaviour won him the gratitude of the Shi'as: the taxi driver looked at me in a kindly way when I referred to the story and made a conciliatory detour to save the life of a lizard at the risk of our own. "You know our history," he said. It was far more vivid to him than the story of Calvary is to most taxi-drivers in London—perhaps because the land and its circumstances have fundamentally not changed, and nothing less monotonous than bloodshed has intervened.

Nejf has taken the place of Kufa: and though the inhabitants have become settled in the course of time, and gained a good deal of Persian and lost much of the Beduin, it is still a desert city, encircled in a wall and lifted on a low cliff like a crown surmounted by the shiny gold of its dome; the Beduin of the Anezah and Shammar still come to it for provisions from the far sands of the Nefud; and motor lorries and cars take the road to Mekka, the Tariq Zobaida, the Pilgrim way.

As you stand on the height by the city wall, you can see it fade dim and white across a flat green foreground into the haze of Arabia, and can meditate as you feel inclined either on the pilgrim feet that through centuries have walked in hope the dust of that difficult highway, or on the constant shuttle of intrigue that ever ran to and fro between the Centres of Religion and the conquered eastern lands.

I find both these subjects of meditation equally fascinating. But with that invisible horizon before me, so clear to the eye of faith, I could not but stand reverent before the devotion of man—with a passing wonder at those of our politicians who think they can hold the hearts of people by material means alone. Perhaps they have never stood on the hill of Nejf and seen the Pilgrim road. Small donkeys, with brushwood trailing from their panniers in the dust on either side of them, were climbing up the hill: a few buildings stood in the hollow like little forts—really nothing more warlike than the homes of the Nejf tannery industry. Looking down from my bare hillock on the other side, I saw the wall of Nejf immediately below, hemming in the close-packed houses round their shrine.

I spent a week in Nejf, in the hospitable modernity of the

Nejf

Qaimaqam's guest house, of which, and of my host, I have a
kind and happy memory. It was near the Young Men's Club,
which possesses the desert town's only walled garden, filled
with oleanders and mud-banked rivulets, where the progres-
sive young men sit about and talk in the afternoon.

Husain, who had been lent me as a servant, looked after me
and the club simultaneously, and used to put me in a secluded
corner of the garden, with the result that, after a day or two
of gazing, the whole club came in a body to my little house to
call, their chairs carried after them and arranged in a semi-
circle round me, just as I woke from my afternoon sleep.

They were pleasant young men, all passionately modern, all
devoted to education in a disinterested, ardent way typical of
Nejf, which has pursued learning for its own sake through the
ages. The objects are altered, but the spirit remains: the young
men's allegiance is given to their secondary school and the
task of building a new European nation out of their ancient
land: they were pained because I had been seen photograph-
ing a miserable weaver at a hand-loom in his shop. I knew it
was useless to explain that the beauty of the secondary school
is of that spiritual kind that does not appeal to the photog-
rapher: I apologized for my taste, and tried to shield it by
describing how Europe, now rapidly returning to the Dark
Ages, is coming to prefer handicrafts to the machine. One
machine-loom in Nejf, I explained, would take away the live-
lihood of all the weavers of the town. Seen in a truly modern
light, the old weaver stands in the van of Progress. The Intelligentsia of Nejf took the explanation kindly but with a lin-
gering doubt. It is hard if European fashions in civilization are
going to change before the Eastern version has time to get
going.

At lunch and dinner I sat opposite the Qaimaqam in a cool
cellar or *sirdab* of his, to which a subterranean well far below
gave, through an opening in the floor, a dank sort of coolness.
With a variety of excellent stews between us, we used to

discuss modern problems and the improvement of Nejf, which he attends to with fatherly care.

He was a charming man, with the simplicity in him of a life begun in the army, and a philosophy engendered by years of administration, a combination which produces much the same pleasant type in an Iraqi as an Englishman. The former must perhaps develop a little more philosophy than the latter, and therefore a more tolerant attitude towards himself and the world in general. There is no doubt that an Eastern governor comes to know a great deal about human nature, which makes him agreable to talk to. My Qaimaqam, too, had come to it by way of the police, and not by that substitute for human knowledge—the scholastic examination: he still thought lovingly of his open life with the desert patrols, better than his office chair in the *serai*: "and when I am old," he said unexpectedly, for he was a man of affairs and a practical man, "I should like to come and sit in a library in Nejf, and wear a black abba and white turban, and study Religion.

"To-morrow," he said one day, "I will take you to see our religious Head, Shaikh Muhammad 'Abdu'l-Husain al-Ghata', whose fathers before him for five generations have been our leaders in this town."

He took me accordingly—after some little consultation as to the least conspicuous hour, for the visit of a woman smacks somewhat of frivolity. Shaikh Hadi, who copies books which Nejf still passes from hand to hand in manuscript, came first to look at me, and having sent in a favourable report, took us through winding alleys to an unobtrusive house where, like the early Moslems in unpretentious simplicity, the Shaikh lives among his people. We climbed through a plain narrow door up a high narrow stair, to a barely furnished room on the roof—two cotton mattresses and a rug on the floor, and an old servant offering cigarettes: and presently saw the Shaikh himself appear, preceded through the narrow door by an immense white turban, under which his lean face and bright henna beard looked like a Persian miniature, extremely dignified. He is an old man, but with a mouth so mobile, impish, and intelligent, so quick a twinkle in his eye, that age can have little hold upon his spirit. He gave me the tips of his fingers, and sat down with that nuance of velvet authority which is recognizably ecclesiastical the world over.

In his time he had known Gertrude Bell and Sir Percy Cox and considered all were lesser people who came after: and, speaking of what now occupies the Eastern world, told me his opinion on Britain and Islam. "There is nothing now but friendship," he said, "between us and the English, if it were not for the wrongs of our Arab brothers in Palestine: and while those last, there can be neither peace nor love between us from the Mediterranean to India. And this I hope you will tell your government, and tell them that what they are playing with is not the little land of Palestine, but the whole world of Islam, which is half their empire, and now longs for friendship with them and possibly protection." As this happens to coincide with my own view of a delicate question, I was glad to promise Shaikh 'Abdu'l-Husain to do my best to repeat his words; and soon left him, and walked back through the bazaar, busy with morning traffic and fluttering wings of pigeons in its dim upper recesses pin-pricked with light.

The Qaimaqam always took me about in the mornings, or sent me with Husain as escort to see the new things he had made—the open square and garden where the old gate used to be, the two girls' schools started with some struggle in the face of prejudice—the breach in the walls where the new boulevard will greet the traveller from Kerbela. I suggested an archway to ornament the breach and his name and date written in coloured tiles upon it, so that he might be honoured in his works and the effect of the great wall and its buttresses, jutting out among the cupolas and blue glazed domes of graves, might not be lost.

There on your right hand as you come into the town is one

of the three little houses where bodies are washed before their burial. An open place, with melon plants growing across a portico, leads to two inner rooms where a stone slab lies beside a cistern and tap of running water above. A man and his sister live there and deal with the male and female dead at one rupee per body—cheap, considering that some of the corpses come from Afghanistan: these, however, have been prepared in their own homes and are no longer brought in a state of decomposition as they used a few years ago: but they still come from all over Iraq, and the water they are washed with drains away, seemingly among the Nejf wells, so that I felt happy to think that what I was drinking comes in pipes from the Qaimaqam's hygienic new supply.

I used to wander of an evening outside the town, under this great wall in the dusk, and admire the new moon hanging above the windowless buttress in a daffodil sky. The women and children of Nejf took the air then and sat about their graves. Their city of the dead drifts out into the desert—no walls are needed there.

Inside the walls, winding lanes lead converging to one or other gateway of the Shrine.

One evening I spent watching the great gate of the Shrine, and the fading of the light upon it, and remember it as one of the most beautiful evenings of my life. A small open space there, surrounded by booths and shopkeepers, separates the Shrine from the bazaar. Most of these people had become friendly by this time. The first day, when I photographed the gate, a little outcry arose because I could look into the inner court: I saw a fat man, the chief fomenter of trouble, went up to him where he sold aluminium cooking-pots, and explained that what I wanted was pictures of the pilgrims, not the Shrine, "Could I take them sideways from his shop?"

After that all was well. We bowed to each other the next night across the busy little space, and he presently came up to ask if Nejf pleased me. The police have a small room here made all of windows just above the level of the pavement; they put me there with the windows open, so that I was almost but not quite in the street: five henna-bearded old men sat on a bench below, smoking one hookah between them; they turned their heads now and then to me, and gradually smiled. The people crowded in a constant stream, in and out of the darkness of their door: the shadow of its arch was less black in the evening light; the electric lamps that surround the window of carved brickwork began to shine and made the wall, its flowered tiles and gold, glow softly like a garden of roses.

In the inner court, against a gold background, the prayer was preparing; the muezzin's voice could just be heard above the chatter of the outer piazza. Water carriers now brought their donkeys, unloaded the heavy skins on to their hips with a loop of rope to balance and catch the outer corner, and stepped into the Shrine. The money-changers sat in their two booths and counted out the gains of the day. The shops of the piazza—tobacco, rosaries, striped silks from Damascus and aniline from Europe—were more or less idle, but a great business was doing in coffee; a young man in a red apron stood on one foot and clinked each little cup twice against the beak of the coffee pot as he poured, just for style. A sofa and two armchairs from the furniture shop, blue velvet flowers on a mustard ground, were put full out in the open for public use before being sold; and an old man near them on the ground sat selling skull-caps, and let the traffic divide around him. It poured on constantly, stepping across the high threshold— men in abbas, some carelessly askew with a *keffiah* above, some straight and tidy with a turban, black for the servants of the Shrine, white for the students of religion, green for the descendants of the Prophet: the red Sunni *keffiah* is not seen here; but sometimes a *sidara* which the policemen who wear it "turn to the back of our head as we go in so that the star of Iraq may not be above us when we come before the Imam."

The Persians, who have the Shah in the lining of their hats, have to take them off altogether if they wish to be respectful. A coffin came along, open and shallow, with a body wrapped in red and yellow, just washed and being carried before burial round the tomb. The labour of life is not over for the religious dead; they are taken first to visit the two shrines of Kerbela, loaded on a taxi across the desert of the lizards with their relatives on the back seat, then washed, taken round the tomb of Nejf, and finally laid according to their means nearer or farther from the holy walls. Close behind the coffin came a pedlar, with second-hand abbas over his head and shoulders and a *crêpe de Chine* dress among them. The dusk had fallen: all except the lighted door was dim. The people were praying inside. A row of them stood behind an old imam, who bent and staightened himself in an immense white turban against the background of gold. There was a feeling of peace—something like a cathedral city but less parochial, perhaps because of all this human trafficking outside.

As I came away the long bazaar was lighted, with busy clusters round the coloured crockery of the eating shops. I walked, feeling in love with all the world, and was suddenly shocked to see an old shoemaker cross-legged in his booth staring at me with eyes of concentrated hate. One gets these shocks in Nejf, and it is horrid to be hated all for nothing. And what a strange revelation of self-esteem it is when people only love those who think and feel as they do—an extension of themselves, in fact! Even Christianity does not cure us—since one cannot feel right without assuming that the rest must be wrong. Personally I would rather feel wrong with everybody else than right all by myself: I like people different, and agree with the man who said that the worst of the human race is the number of duplicates: the old shoemaker was wasting his missionary feelings. And if he had been able to look past my English bodice into my heart, he would have seen that what it was filled with at the moment was a friendly respect for his Shrine, which stands over the souls of men as the golden dome of Nejf stands over the desert, and draws them from afar. I was thinking of the ramshackle khan where old Afghans, having walked across the steppes of Asia, pay one rupee a month for a room to live in the neighbourhood of their Holy Place, ready to be gathered finally into its sacred dust. Their *kilims* for prayer are spread in the courtyard; at the door of each little cell, under a dilapidated wooden colonnade, an earthen jar in a wooden frame drips water-drops from its pointed base into a bowl: and that is all their furniture, more or less. They eke out a living by weaving black wool for tents, staked out on the ground between the *kilims*; and meet once a week for a "service of remembrance" when, out of their poverty, they scrape each a *fils* (the fiftieth of a shilling) and send it to the Shrine. Who are we to criticize a faith that gives so much?

"God be their guide from camp to camp: God be their shade from well to well;
God grant beneath the desert stars they hear the Prophet's camel bell.

"And, son of Islam, it may be that thou shalt learn at journey's end
Who walks thy garden eve on eve, and bows his head, and calls thee Friend."